FROM GHETTO TO EMANCIPATION:

HISTORICAL AND CONTEMPORARY RECONSIDERATIONS OF THE JEWISH COMMUNITY

FROM GHETTO TO EMANCIPATION:

HISTORICAL AND CONTEMPORARY RECONSIDERATIONS OF THE JEWISH COMMUNITY

Edited by

David N. Myers and William V. Rowe

SCRANTON: UNIVERSITY OF SCRANTON PRESS

Library of Congress Cataloging-In-Publication Data

From ghetto to emancipation : historical and contemporary
  reconsiderations of the Jewish community / edited by David N. Myers
and William V. Rowe.
     p.   cm.
    Includes bibliographical references and index.
    ISBN 0-940866-72-2 (hc). -- ISBN 0-940866-73-0 (pbk.)
    1. Jews--Cultural assimilation--Congresses. 2. Jews--Segregation-
-Congresses. 3. Jews--Politics and government--1948- --Congresses.
4. Jews--Pennsylvania--Scranton--Congresses. I. Myers, David N.
II. Rowe, William V., 1951- .
DS148.F77   1997
305.892'4--dc21   97-40037
                                                  CIP

Distribution:

University of Scranton Press
Chicago Distribution Center
11030 S. Langley
Chicago IL 60628

CONTENTS

INTRODUCTION

David N. Myers

It was some seventy years ago, in 1928, that Salo Wittmayer Baron, then a young Jewish historian, published a provocative essay, "Ghetto and Emancipation," whose echoes continue to reverberate powerfully to this day. This early essay contains in concentrated form many of the important themes that would mark Baron's thought throughout his extraordinary career.[1] The urgent desire to abandon an excessively gloomy view of Jewish history, which Baron designated the "lachrymose conception" of Jewish history, makes its first appearance in the concluding line of "Ghetto and Emancipation."[2] Baron was especially intent on overturning the "traditional view" alluded to in the article's subtitle—the ubiquitous distinction made by Jewish historians between "the black of the Jewish Middle Ages and the white of the post-Emancipation period . . ."[3] According to Baron, this historiographical tendency, born in the formative generations of Jewish historiography in nineteenth-century Germany, was woefully misleading. The Jewish Middle Ages were not a source of unending misery. Not only did medieval Jews possess "more rights than the great bulk of the population," but the Jewish community "enjoyed full internal autonomy."[4] This latter privilege issued naturally from the corporatist order of medieval feudalism. Conversely, it stood in direct conflict with modern theories of governance in which the State demanded a direct relationship with the individual subject-citizen. Ironically, Baron couples his retreat from the lachrymose conception of the Jewish Middle Ages with a decidedly lachrymose view of Jewish modernity. Indeed, he takes fierce exception to those Jewish historians who celebrate the advent of Jewish political emancipation as "the dawn of a new day after a nightmare of the deepest horror."[5]

Baron's strictures in "Ghetto and Emancipation" point to the disturbing and disabling effects of the emancipatory process: the loss of communal autonomy, the assumption of new and onerous obligations imposed by the state, the evisceration of the national component of Jewish identity, and the recasting of Judaism into a narrow confessional mold. Hovering above Baron's essay is the spirit of Count Clermont-Tonnere, a delegate to the French National Assembly, who declared in 1789 that "the Jews should be denied everything as a nation, but granted everything as individuals." This statement epitomizes Baron's sense of the deep structural flaws of Jewish modernity—specifically, the imperative to surrender all but the most meager vestiges of communal identity in return for individual political rights.[6]

Of course, Baron was hardly the first thinker in modern times to call attention to the hazards of emancipation. Reticence about a new transformative politics surfaced in the midst of the very Enlightenment movements that agitated for it. Such diverse eighteenth-century figures as Rousseau, Burke, and Hamann shared a concern over the loss of tradition, community, and a secure sense of the past, which was seemingly mandated by the new liberal creed. For some, such as the German Counter-Enlightenment thinker Johann David Michaelis, it was the emancipation of the Jews itself that signaled the corrupting influence of liberalism on German group integrity.[7]

Notwithstanding these conservative critiques, the tenets of political liberalism not only were validated by the French Revolution, but served more broadly as pillars for a sweeping process of *embourgeoisement* in nineteenth-century Europe. And yet, voices of dissent were never stifled. In fact, Carl Schorske notes the irony that in Austria in the last quarter of the nineteenth century, "the program which the liberals had devised against the upper classes occasioned the explosion of the lower."[8] The resulting radicalization led to a dizzying proliferation of new anti-liberal ideologies—socialism, ultra-nationalism, anti-Semitism—all of which were sounded in a shriller and "sharper key" than previous political expressions.[9]

To the extent that no group had invested more faith and goodwill in the Enlightenment project than the Jews, the resulting "failure of liberalism left the Jew a victim."[10] One of the most noteworthy Jewish "victims" was Theodor Herzl, whose grandiose vision of cultural ecumenism between Jews and Europeans was shattered by the Dreyfus Affair in 1894. For Herzl, the Jewish response to the anti-Dreyfusards—and the unfortunate but inevitable response to Count Clermont-Tonnere—was to affirm precisely that which had been discarded one hundred years earlier: Jewish national identity. The

Zionist program announced in Herzl's *Der Judenstaat* of 1896 was thus a blueprint for a reconstituted Jewish national community. Even though the political form of this community was to resemble a bourgeois Central European state, Herzl's Zionism demanded the end of Jewish existence in Europe, and thus signaled the loss of a certain liberal innocence for the Jews.

Salo Baron knew well the formative Viennese environment in which Theodor Herzl's illusions were fostered. Baron studied at the city's university, where he earned three doctorates. He was well aware of the city's longstanding infatuation with anti-Semitism, epitomized by the election of Karl Lueger as mayor in 1895. No doubt, he was also aware of the ironic effects of anti-Semitism in reversing the Jewish march to assimilation. Yet, he did not choose to follow in Herzl's Zionist footsteps. Nor did he give voice to the negative consequences of the Jewish entry into modernity while in Vienna. Rather, he wrote "Ghetto and Emancipation" in New York, far from the highly charged environment of Central Europe. America clearly offered a more stable Jewish environment than Europe to him and many others. But it possessed its own, more subtle dangers. Indeed, it was precisely the absence of a deeply rooted anti-Semitic political culture in America that intensified the appeal of social integration for Jews.[11] Conversely, it was the imperative of assimilation, as reflected in the pervasive metaphor of the melting pot, that threatened the strong communal, ethnic, and religious loyalties of new Americans. From this perspective, New York of the 1920s was a quite logical venue in which to confront the perils of assimilation, if not the larger triumphalist myth of Jewish modernity.

Baron's concerns were not expressed in a conceptual vacuum. A series of trenchant American critics had expressed dissatisfaction with the "melting pot" model for at least a decade. Indeed, cultural pluralists like Horace M. Kallen, Randolph Bourne, and Judah L. Magnes refused to surrender the potential benefit of group rights. They preferred the model of a "symphony" of nationalities over the "melting pot," cognizant that liberal "democracy has the tendency to level all distinctions, to create the average type, almost to demand uniformity."[12] Baron stood upon this foundation of criticism in "Ghetto and Emancipation." Unlike the cultural pluralists, he offered no political prescriptions. But he did share their fears about the insidious consequences of apparently benevolent processes of social amelioration. He exhibited these fears in a brief historical essay with judgments as sweeping and reductionist as those against which he inveighed. Indeed, while challenging the sharp and value-laden dichotomy between premodern and modern Jewish history, Baron substituted his own, somewhat counterintuitive contrast; his version of modernity became a sort of Dark Age for the Jews both in terms of their communal identity and their physical well-being.

If Baron overstated his case at times, his considerable erudition also led him to important insights in "Ghetto and Emancipation." In particular, he identified the emancipatory process not merely as the beginning of Jewish modernity, but as the site of a new and tension-filled social contract. Under this arrangement, the Jews stood to lose much—the very core of their group identity—in receiving rights of citizenship. This exchange prompted Baron to observe that "emancipation was a necessity even more for the modern State than for Jewry."[13] Lurking beneath the benign rhetoric of liberalism was a concerted agenda of coercion.

Many have followed Baron's direction, most without knowing or acknowledging his contribution. A particularly intriguing line of inquiry has linked the totalitarian manifestations of the twentieth century, fascism and Nazism, to intellectual and social transformations in the eighteenth century. In their famous indictment in *Dialectic of Enlightenment*, Horkheimer and Adorno denounced the "repressive equality" that had its source in the Enlightenment.[14] The two German émigrés attempted to uncover the way in which state action could be and was justified in the name of the exalted ideal of reason—to the exclusion of any enduring moral principles.

More recent thinkers such as the Frenchmen Emmanuel Levinas, Michel Foucault, Jean-François Lyotard, and Jacques Derrida have further challenged the Enlightenment legacy by questioning its hyper-rationality. They share a deep skepticism about the Enlightenment "metanarrative" in which "the hero of knowledge works toward a good ethico-political end—universal peace."[15] In their challenge to the core Enlightenment precepts of progress and human reason, these thinkers have ushered in a new moment of reflection on the project of modernity itself. According to Lyotard, this moment, marked by a decided "incredulity toward metanarratives," merits the designation postmodern.[16] It is in this postmodern age (though not always of it) that searching reconsiderations of the liberal ideal in American society have come from a wide array of thinkers ranging from Richard Rorty to Alasdair MacIntyre to Michael Sandel. One important outgrowth has been a neo-communitarian ethos in American social and political thought focused on the reinvigoration of civic virtue and responsibility.[17]

A related though distinct perspective advocates "a consistent and principled approach to minority rights" within a liberal democratic order.[18] These various political conceptions reflect an ongoing struggle at the end of the twentieth century to address a question posed two centuries earlier: how can a group seeking to preserve a measure of collective identity survive within a liberal society that values individual rights and obligations above all else? It is this question that Salo Baron so starkly formulated regarding the Jewish community in his "Ghetto and Emancipation." And it is this question to which the current volume offers a response, or series of fruitfully diverse responses.

II

The origins of this volume are perhaps more mystifying than the central problem which it engages. One would not necessarily expect that the grand issues of modern Jewish identity would win a hearing at a Jesuit university in a small American city whose Jewish community numbers between three and four thousand souls. And yet, it was at the University of Scranton that a conference entitled "From Ghetto to Emancipation: Historical and Contemporary Reconsiderations of the Jewish Community" was held in March 1995. The conference attracted a distinguished roster of scholars in various fields of Jewish studies from across the United States, as well as interested faculty from the host University of Scranton.

The impetus for a major conference in the field of Jewish studies at the University of Scranton came from Rabbi Dr. David Geffen. Since moving to Scranton to assume a pulpit there some five years ago, Rabbi Geffen has infused a new spirit and intellectual vitality into the local Jewish community. Several years ago, he seized upon the idea of an important scholarly event to mark the fiftieth anniversary of the Scranton-Lackawanna Jewish Federation. After a series of discussions, he entrusted the task of carrying the plan forward to me, a native of Scranton and a product of its Jewish community.

Rabbi Geffen's idea presented me with an opportunity not only to return to my hometown, but to revisit the predicament of the Jewish community in the modern age. Growing up in the 1960s and 1970s, I remember Jewish Scranton as a community of tight-knit social and family relations, of well-established institutions, and of a clearly defined sense of group distinctiveness. In visits back over the past decade and a half, I have encountered a shadow of the community's former self.

This is particularly true for the once-dominant non-Orthodox segment—though much less so for the Orthodox segment which is currently experiencing a demographic renaissance. However, most members of the age cohort with whom I grew up have chosen to leave the embracing confines of the Scranton community for a wider world, lured by new educational and professional prospects. The result has been a "graying" of large sectors of the community, prompting its leaders to ponder the prospects for continued existence. Their concerns are hardly unique. On the contrary, they mirror the concerns of the broader American Jewish community for which assimilation appears as the chief social ill.

When thinking back upon my childhood in Scranton, I do not conjure up romantic images of a seamlessly holistic community. Instead, what I recall is the pervasive tension that defined me as a member of a group whose boundaries were both readily identifiable and yet permeable. Social relations between Jews and non-Jews, indeed, between Jews and Jesuits, were so normal as to merit no special attention. This was the norm for at least three generations, extending back to my grandparents. And yet, each of the generations possessed an unmistakable sense of membership in the "community," affirmed not only by the defining institutions of synagogue, community center, and charitable organization, but also by the conscious acknowledgment of the wider non-Jewish world with which we regularly interacted.

The Scranton experience suggests an important qualification to Salo Baron's sharp dichotomy between ghetto and emancipation. Perhaps the two phenomena, ghetto and emancipation, need not be seen in opposition. Perhaps the process of political emancipation, and the very project of modernity itself, were not solely a matter of surrender to the leveling force of liberalism. Perhaps these processes had a far more ambiguous character, leading to a multiplicity of outcomes other than the inexorable demise of group identities. In this regard, one recalls Jürgen Habermas, whose defense of the project of modernity is "a plea for the maintenance of its dialectical tensions, rather than for their overcoming in a perfectly Enlightened form of life."[19]

The essays in this volume investigate these tensions from a variety of illuminating perspectives. David B. Ruderman commences his evocative paper on "The Cultural Significance of the Ghetto in Jewish History" by questioning whether the shift from ghetto to emancipation meant moving "from an inherently bad condition . . . to a good one . . ."[20] Ruderman then proceeds with a brief history of the ghetto idea in Jewish thought and historiography, culminating with a critique of the gifted historian of Italian Jewry, Robert Bonfil. Ruderman eschews Bonfil's internalist approach with its emphasis on the immanent allure and creative power of the ghetto environment. He does not dispute that the ghetto afforded "a sense of Jewish space where Jews retained a vital feeling of group solidarity and cultural autonomy." But the ghetto was also the arena for "a constant and intense cultural negotiation and dialogue with the outside world."[21]

This important thematic thread in Ruderman's discussion of early modern Jewish history is picked up in my own contribution to this volume, "'The Blessing of Assimilation' Reconsidered." My paper draws its inspiration from a largely forgotten lecture delivered by Gerson Cohen in 1966 in which the eminent scholar called attention to the unavoidable and even salutary effects of assimilation in Jewish history. Rather than dismiss the assimilatory process as an unmitigated evil, Cohen, and I in his wake, suggest that assimilation can and must be seen as an important source of cultural exchange and, hence, vitality. I explore this idea in the context of modern Jewish history, mindful of the fact that a similar understanding of assimilation prevails in the current cultural studies discourse of diaspora and transnational identities. My paper aims to induce a dialogue across fields revolving around the multilayered notion of assimilation.

Though not directly interrogating the idea of assimilation, Michael L. Morgan focuses upon a group of highly influential and assimilated Central European Jewish thinkers in "Redemption and Community: Reflections on Some European Jewish Intellectuals, 1900–1940." In this wide-ranging essay, Morgan attempts to trace a discursive tradition in which the themes of community and redemption stand in constant and productive tension. This tradition is located at the juncture of two important currents in early twentieth-century Central European history: the pervasive concern with community that followed Ferdinand Tönnies' renowned *Gemeinschaft und Gesellschaft* of 1887; and the bold new forms of messianic, and often apocalyptic, expressions to which leading intellectuals gave voice.[22] While exposing the divergent perspectives of such figures as Georg Simmel, Martin Buber, Georg Lukacs, and Franz Kafka, Morgan notes their shared desire to confront the "crisis of modern culture" through the categories of community and redemption.

William V. Rowe's "Difficult Freedom: The Basis of Community in Emmanuel Levinas" is an interesting sequel to Morgan's presentation. Similarly concerned with the link between redemption and community,

Rowe's inquiry into Levinas marks a passage from German to French thought, and thereby retraces Levinas' own role in introducing important German philosophers (i.e., Husserl and Heidegger) into France. Rowe carefully excavates three layers of connotations of "ghetto" in Levinas' thought: the first (and most traditional) signifies the largely autonomous *pre-modern* Jewish community; the second alludes to the *modern* ghetto of alienation created by the emancipatory process; and the third refers to the "reactionary and anti-semitic ghetto that is based on the failure of emancipation." Taking a cue from Salo Baron, Rowe concentrates on the second ghetto which "represented the effective isolation not of Jews, but of their Judaism, from Western life and even from the lives of emancipated Jews themselves." He analyzes Levinas' diagnosis of and prescription for this ghetto predicament. Rowe suggests that for Levinas, a meaningful community, based on "true sociality," must embody "the infinity of responsibility for the Other." Indeed, it is in this responsibility that the possibility for a new, nontotalitarian universality—antidote to the ghetto of modernity—inheres.

Nomi M. Stolzenberg shifts the focus from post-Holocaust French intellectual discourse to contemporary American legal thought in "The Puzzling Persistence of Community: The Cases of Airmont and Kiryas Joel." Her concern is the fate of communal aspirations within the constitutional order of the United States; the prism through which she contemplates this fate is the case of Kiryas Joel, a Satmar Hasidic Jewish community in upstate New York, whose residents appealed to the state to support the incorporation of a public school for its disabled children. While tracing the legal battle over such support all the way to the Supreme Court, Stolzenberg juxtaposes the case of Kiryas Joel to that of Airmont, another New York community which sought to prevent Orthodox Jews from establishing informal prayer assemblies in their homes. At the heart of this juxtaposition is Stolzenberg's interest in the very nature of liberalism, whose core principles of neutrality and tolerance seem antithetical to the continued existence of insular, perhaps even intolerant, communities. Her analysis suggests that "liberalism is a rich and variegated tradition" which, contrary to conventional understanding, allows for the possibility of homogeneous communities "exercis(ing) political power for their own ends."

Stolzenberg's presentation of the struggle to preserve communal integrity in the face of social and legal obstacles is an excellent theoretical complement to Arthur A. Goren's rich historical essay, "The Rites of Community, The Public Culture of American Jews." Delivered as the 1995 Morris B. Gelb Memorial Lecture, Goren's paper examines the way in which Jewish immigrants to the United States sought to invent new forms of communal identity in their transplanted homeland. In particular, he focuses on the rituals of mourning and celebration which American Jews, primarily in the early twentieth century, developed in order to foster a stronger sense of communal self-worth. Pervading Goren's analysis is a sense of the loss of textured bonds of group identity which immigration to the United States entailed for millions of Jews. In their absence, American Jews fashioned their own distinct forms of commemoration as a way of validating their communal existence. In the process, a Jewish public culture, "fragile and fluid," was created which served as "an important arena for self-definition."

The final paper in this volume is a doubly fitting conclusion to a volume on the predicament of the modern Jewish community. Michael Brown's "Towards a History of Scranton Jewry" sheds light on the patterns and tensions shaping a small Jewish community in the alternately alluring and threatening American environment. That the focus is upon Scranton—and, moreover, that Professor Brown is a former Scrantonian—seem especially appropriate. Though not a participant in the 1995 conference at the University of Scranton, Professor Brown graciously agreed to include his paper on the history of Scranton's Jewish community in this book. His paper skillfully mixes primary research, oral history, and conceptual rigor, and thereby serves as an excellent model for local history. Further, it provides an arena in which to explore in concrete fashion the larger abstract problems addressed in this volume's diverse and illuminating meditations on Baron's "Ghetto and Emancipation."

III

The final task of this introduction is to thank those who made the conference, and especially this volume, not merely possible but an enormously stimulating and enjoyable pursuit. As I have already indicated, the original inspiration came from Rabbi David Geffen to whom I remain deeply indebted. At early stages of planning, vital assistance in conceiving and organizing the conference came from Sondra Myers. The Scranton-Lackawanna Jewish Federation and its executive director, Seymour Brotman, were enthusiastic proponents of the conference throughout the entire process. In addition, the conference and volume won the unstinting support of the University of Scranton's administration, particularly the President, Rev. J. A. Panuska, S. J., Provost Richard H. Passon, and Dean Paul F. Fahey. It is both a pleasure and a privilege to thank Robert J. Sylvester, Vice President for Institutional Advancement, and Alan Mazzei, Director of Corporate and Foundation Relations, for their indefatigable efforts. Alan, in particular, labored above and beyond the call of duty to assure the success of this undertaking. On the whole, the University of Scranton's commitment to the conference idea, and to Jewish studies more generally, reflects the genuinely catholic interests of these fine individuals and the institution they serve so well.

Among the conference's participants, it is necessary to single out Professors Elisheva Carlebach and Rela Geffen, both of whom offered important intellectual contributions to the proceedings. The conference was also graced by the presence of Shoshana Cardin, distinguished national Jewish leader, whose insights proved stimulating to all in attendance. Mention must also be made of Professor Alan Mittleman of Muhlenberg College for his trenchant critique of my and Professor Stolzenberg's papers. I would also like to thank Professors Harold Baillie and David Friedrichs of the University of Scranton for agreeing to chair two of the conference's sessions.

Vital financial support for the conference and volume has come from many individuals and institutions. Among those who kindly offered assistance were Irwin E. Alperin, Myer M. Alperin, Arley Wholesale, Inc., Herbert Barton, Richard S. Bishop, Kathy and Seymour Brotman, Janice and Harris Cutler, David M. Epstein, Rabbi David Geffen, Mae S. Gelb, The Golub Foundation, The Grossman Family Foundation, Beverly and Jerome Klein, Bertram M. Linder, Ann and I. Leo Moskovitz, Libbye Myers, Sondra and Morey Myers, Paul Rosenberg, Dr. Stephen I. Rosenthal, The Robert Saligman Charitable Foundation, Lewis B. Sare, The Scranton-Lackawanna Jewish Federation, Margaret and Douglas Sheldon, Reva and Harold Sprung, The Samuel Tabas Family Foundation, G. Weinberger Company, and The Isaac Ziegler Charitable Trust.

The University of Scranton Press and its director, Father Richard W. Rousseau, S. J., have provided a most hospitable and professional home for this volume. But the volume would not have seen the light of day were it not for Stephanie Chasin. With her keen editorial eye and astounding efficiency, she helped transform a series of conference papers into essays that stand on their own intellectual and stylistic merit. Penultimately, Bill Rowe has proved to be a wonderful collaborator and conversation partner, even in the midst of rather mundane editorial discussions.

Finally, this volume is dedicated to the Jewish community of Scranton whose generosity far exceeds its numbers and whose history brings to life the fascinating and tension-filled predicament of the Jewish community in modern times.

NOTES

1.   Salo Baron, "Ghetto and Emancipation: Shall We Revise the Traditional View?," *The Menorah Journal* 14 (June 1928), 515–526.

2.   Baron refers to the "lachrymose theory" in this final line. "Ghetto and Emancipation," 526. See the analysis of Robert Liberles in his biography, *Salo Wittmayer Baron: Architect of Jewish History* (New York, 1995), 40–45, 340.

3.   Baron, "Ghetto and Emancipation," 517.

4.   Baron, "Ghetto and Emancipation," 518, 520.

5.   Baron, "Ghetto and Emancipation," 517.

6.   Baron, "Ghetto and Emancipation," 524.

7.   See Michaelis' response to the pro-emancipatory pamphlet of C. W. Dohm, *Ueber die buergerliche Verbesserung der Juden* in Paul Mendes-Flohr and Jehuda Reinharz, eds., *The Jew in the Modern World* (New York, 1980), 36–38.

8.   Carl E. Schorske, *Fin-de-Siècle Vienna: Politics and Culture* (New York, 1980), 117.

9.   Schorske defines this new key as "a mode of political behaviour at once more abrasive, more creative, and more satisfying to the life of feeling than the deliberative style of the liberal." *Fin-de-Siècle Vienna,* 119.

10.   Ibid., 118.

11.   This is not to suggest that anti-Semitism did not exist, and at times in powerful doses, in the United States. See, for instance, Leonard Dinnerstein, *Antisemitism in America* (New York, 1994). It is rather to suggest that anti-Semitism was not an ingrained part of the social and political landscape of America as it was in Central Europe in the late nineteenth and early twentieth centuries.

12.   See Judah L. Magnes, "A Republic of Nationalities," in Mendes-Flohr and Reinharz, *The Jew in the Modern World,* 390.

13.   "Ghetto and Emancipation," 524.

14.   Max Horkheimer and Theodor Adorno, *Dialectic of Enlightenment,* translated by John Cummings (New York, 1972), 13.

15. Lyotard, *The Postmodern Condition: A Report on Knowledge*, translated by Geoff Bennington and Brian Massumi (Minneapolis, 1984), xxiv.

16. Ibid., xxiv.

17. See, for example, Amitai Etzioni, *A Spirit of Community: Rights, Responsibilities, and the Communitarian Agenda* (New York, 1993).

18. See Will Kymlicka, *Multicultural Citizenship: A Liberal Theory of Minority Rights* (Oxford, 1995), 195.

19. See Martin Jay's review of Habermas' *The Philosophical Defense of Modernity* in *History and Theory*, 28 (1989), 95.

20. See Ruderman, "The Cultural Significance of the Ghetto in Jewish History," 1.

21. Ruderman, 13.

22. See Ferdinand Tönnies, *Gemeinschaft und Gesellschaft* (Leipzig, 1935). On the neo-messianic expression, see Michael Löwy, *Redemption et utopie: Le judaisme libertaire en Europe centrale* (Paris, 1988).

THE CULTURAL SIGNIFICANCE OF THE GHETTO IN JEWISH HISTORY[1]

David B. Ruderman

S urely one way of understanding the title of our distinguished conference, "From Ghetto to Emancipation," is the conventional way.[2] One might assume that the direction of our deliberations should lead from an inherently bad condition, designated by the term "ghetto," to a good one, leading to a desirable state of freedom. This trajectory follows that of most standard accounts of the Jewish experience: Jews who had lived a "ghettoized" existence were finally "emancipated" in the modern era, and despite the negative consequences of their liberation and integration within Western secular cultures—virulent anti-Semitism and genocide—their emancipated state was surely a boon in comparison with the hermetically sealed and alienated existence of their preliberated state. And indeed, for most modern Jews, the term "ghetto" is laden with similar negative connotations. Such expressions as "the age of ghetto," "ghetto mentality," "ghetto Jew," "out of the ghetto," all imply a highly negative existence, a throwback to an era when Jews were legally and socially restricted and when their culture revealed narrow and pedestrian features, clearly the result of their sequestration. The term "ghetto" has now assumed an even more general designation for neighborhoods densely inhabited by members of minority groups, such as African-Americans or Native Americans, who are forced to live in miserable and deprived conditions because of socioeconomic restraints as well as legal ones.[3]

I would like to discuss the "ghetto" in its historical context in this short essay based on recent scholarship on the subject, which obliges us to reassess its cultural significance for the history of early modern Jewry. This reevaluation, in turn, might shed new light on the notion of ghettoization within a contemporary Jewish context. In short, was the

1

ghetto good or bad for the Jews and the perpetuation of Jewish culture, and what might we learn from the example of the past, if anything, in reflecting upon contemporary Jewish dilemmas?

Although the word "ghetto" was probably first employed to describe a compulsory residential quarter for Jews in Venice established in 1516 on the site of a foundry (*getto*), the "age of the ghetto" in Italy is usually dated some forty years later. In those years, the Jews of the Papal States, together with those in the rest of the Italian peninsula, experienced a radical deterioration in their legal status and physical state due to a new aggressive policy instituted by Pope Paul IV and his successors. Italian Jews suddenly encountered a major offensive against their communities and ancestral heritage. In 1553, tomes of the Talmud were collected in each community and incinerated. In 1555, a ghetto was established in Rome, and the Roman example was gradually emulated in city after city throughout the sixteenth and early seventeenth centuries. By 1569, the Papal States expelled their entire Jewish population with the exception of the communities in Ancona and Rome. The new papal offensive included renewed conversionary activities, especially compulsory appearances by Christian preachers in synagogues and the establishment of transition houses for new converts designed to facilitate large-scale conversion to Christianity. Whether motivated primarily by the need to fortify Christian hegemony against all dissidents, or driven by a renewed missionary zeal for immediate conversion spurred by apocalyptic frenzy, the papacy acted resolutely to undermine the religious life and communal autonomy of those Jews living in the heart of western Christendom.[4]

The centerpiece of the new policy was the ghetto itself, defined simply by Benjamin Ravid as "a compulsory segregated Jewish quarter in which all Jews were required to live and in which no Christians were allowed to live."[5] While Ravid points out that compulsory, segregated, and enclosed Jewish quarters had occasionally existed in Europe prior to the founding of the Venetian one in 1516, this was the first time that the term was used to designate the newly imposed Jewish neighborhoods, and the term continued to gain currency throughout the century. As Kenneth Stow has written, the notion of the ghetto fit perfectly into the overall policy of the new Counter-Reformation papacy. Through enclosure and segregation, the Catholic community was to be shielded most effectively from Jewish contamination. Since Jews could be more easily supervised within a closed quarter, the intense conversionary pressure would prove to be more effective while strict canon law segregating Jews from Christians could be rigidly enforced.

When the ghetto in Rome was enlarged in 1589, Jews even began to refer to it as their *ghet*, possibly ascribing a Hebrew etymology to the Italian term (the Hebrew *get*, meaning divorce). As Stow speculates, the Jews now innately felt that their "divorce" was final, that they were fated to live in a permanent state of subservience and separation from the rest of Christian society.[6]

From the perspective of the standard historical accounts of Italian Jewry, the age of the ghetto stood in sharp contrast to the period that had immediately preceded it, the Renaissance. From the thirteenth century, individual Jews were attracted to settle in the small city-states of northern and central Italy, usually as moneylenders. A small number of them soon became prominent as the economic mainstays of the fledgling Jewish communities in the region and the primary source of communal leadership. These Jewish bankers supported the cultural activities of the Jewish communities in a manner not unlike those of privileged patrons of Christian culture. By the second half of the fifteenth century, recurrent signs of organized Jewish communal activity became more visible. In the same era, immigrants from Germany and southern France joined the original native Italian element in settling these regions. The 1492 expulsion of the Jews from Spain resulted in a new influx of Sephardic Jews, who arrived in Italy as early as 1493. The infusion of larger numbers of Jews into these regions sometimes evoked hostile reactions from elements of the local populace, often fomented by Franciscan preachers who railed incessantly against the insidious effects of Jewish money lending. But this hostility was also counterbalanced by the relatively benign relations that existed between certain Jewish and Christian intellectuals in Italy at the height of the Renaissance and long after. As oft-repeated in the colorful narratives of Cecil Roth, Attilio Milano, or Moses Avigdor Shulvass, a small but conspicuous community of enlightened Jews frequented the courts of Renaissance despots and interacted socially and intellectually with their Christian counterparts. The new openness of the Renaissance created novel opportunities for Jewish-Christian rapprochement, for the infusion of new aesthetic sensibilities among Jewish savants, and for new avenues of Jewish literary creativity and pedagogic reform. Yet despite these new possibilities, the policies of the Counter-Reformation papacy brought to an abrupt end the accomplishments the Renaissance had wrought. The incipient transformations of the Renaissance era were swept away by the new religious zealots. A relatively open society was soon replaced by the closure of the ghetto space. Cultural interaction was cut short by the newly erected walls separating the Jewish from the Christian neighborhoods. And the Jews ultimately had no other recourse than to retreat into their increasingly parochial and stifling ghetto environments.[7]

A recent treatment of the Venetian ghetto by sociologist Richard Sennett continues to view the ghetto experience, in contrast to that of the Renaissance, in similar ways. In a chapter entitled "The Fear of Touching," the author views the ghetto as a kind of urban condom, isolating the Jewish diseases that had infected the Christian community in a prophylactic space. Since Jews were considered synonymous with corrupting bodily vices, sealed barriers separating the impure from the pure were deemed the only means of preserving the spiritual and physical health of the Christian body politic. Sennett does note, however, the irony that Jews did make much out of their very segregation; their ghettos became centers of pride and honor, despite the unpleasant conditions of their imprisonment. This positive sense of self-determination seemingly shaped by the ghetto experience stands in sharp contrast to the more modern "ghettos" tainted with shame and failure. In noting the paradox of feeling good about oneself in a space of degradation, Sennett points in the direction of the rethinking about the ghetto in recent Jewish scholarship, a contradiction already alluded to by Cecil Roth many years earlier.[8] We shall return to the "paradox" of ghetto life below, but before reconsidering the conventional view, I offer four discrete scenes of ghetto life that might serve as a basis for our discussion and analysis of the ghetto experience in Italy, particularly at the end of the sixteenth and the beginning of the seventeenth centuries. By offering concrete glimpses of the culture of the Jewish ghettos, I hope to probe more deeply the paradox which Roth and Sennett noticed and to try and explain it.

In 1638, a distinguished rabbi named Simone Luzzatto, of the ghetto of Venice, composed an apologetic work in Italian and submitted it to the Doge and citizenry of Venice, petitioning them to withdraw a proposal to banish the Jews from living in the city. In a powerful, rhetorical style, studded with quotations from classical writers, Luzzatto gave voice to the sense of entitlement the Jews felt in inhabiting their urban spaces. By the time Luzzatto composed his *Discorso circa il stato gl'Hebrei*, the initial space of the ghetto had grown dramatically in size holding three distinct Jewish populations: the *Tedeschi*, Ashkenazic Jews who had migrated from north-central Europe; the *Levantini*, Jews of Sephardic origin who most recently had entered the Venetian territories from the East via the Ottoman Empire; and the *Ponentini*, recent Converso émigrés from Spain and Portugal who had returned or were candidates for return to the Jewish community and its faith. In the name of all three groups, Luzzatto underscored the political loyalty of Venice's Jewish subjects, the openness and attractiveness of their culture within a Catholic society such as Venice's, and most importantly, the critical commercial role Jews played in the economic life of Venetians which would be severely compromised by their expulsion. Although Jews had written apologetic defenses of their community and faith before Luzzatto's, his work was surely original in its design and its manifest aim; to influence the court of public opinion by demanding the Jewish right to domicile for both ethical reasons and for those related to economic and political policy.[9]

Several years earlier, in 1624, the most illustrious rabbi of Venice, Leone Modena, a close associate of the aforementioned Luzzatto, organized a major celebration in honor of the graduation of his accomplished student Joseph Hamiz, who had just received his medical diploma from the prestigious University of Padua. Taking full advantage of the printing press to publicize his message, as Luzzatto had done, Modena solicited and received numerous congratulatory poems and other messages of commendation in honor of the achievement of his brilliant protégé. This was not the first nor the last time Jewish medical graduates were honored in such a manner. But due to the prestige of Modena and those who added their names and poetic contributions to the pamphlet Modena produced, Hamiz's graduation party represented a special moment of self-adulation for a community which took great pride in its Jewish physicians, particularly those like Hamiz who integrated their medical with traditional rabbinic learning. The prestige and authority of a university degree often assured an enhanced status to an increasing number of rabbis of the Italian ghettos both among Jews and Christians alike. Unanticipated by Modena in his moment of celebration and satisfaction was Hamiz's seemingly bizarre and clearly controversial choice some years later: to abandon his life course of rationalism and science for one fueled by the spiritual energy of the kabbalah and the messianic frenzy surrounding the figure of Shabbetai Zevi. Modena could never understand, in the final analysis, why his most prized student had deserted his teacher's path to "dwell in the garden" of mystical fantasies and apocalyptic delusions. But, in 1624, Modena had no inkling about this strange course of events. Jewish students like Hamiz were entering the university in impressive numbers and they were competing with Christian students successfully, fortifying Jewish intellectual life and enhancing the image of the Jewish communities to which they returned.[10]

Some years earlier, Leone Modena initiated a different but related project to enhance the positive image of Judaism within the Venetian ghetto. He recruited his talented friend, Salamone de'Rossi, to compose music to Hebrew texts, introducing for the first time polyphonic choral performances within the synagogue service. By so doing, Modena was eager to fuse Jewish cultural habits with those of the larger Catholic society. As Dan Harrán has shown, the music was simply a genus, an aesthetic experience neither Jewish nor Christian in itself. Synagogal music became Jewish only when Jewish texts were employed. Not the style of the music but its purpose was critical in legitimating its usage within the sacred space of the synagogue and within the sacred time of Jewish worship. To soften any expected criticism of this audacious transformation of the aesthetics of the traditional worship service, Modena composed a rabbinical responsum arguing that the novelties being introduced were both appropriate and spiritually worthwhile from the perspective of hallowed Jewish practice. Upholding the model of musical innovation in the ancient Biblical Temple and downplaying the break with traditional norms of mournfulness employed since the Temple's destruction, Modena could only imagine the positive benefits that appropriating the artistry of so talented a composer to amplify the spiritual power the synagogue service would convey to its congregation of worshippers.[11]

In stark contrast to the scenes of cultural integration exemplified by Jewish political writing, university graduation, and polyphonic synagogue music, is the following portrait of the ambience of a ghetto. At about the same time that de'Rossi was introducing his new music into the synagogue, a kabbalist of the neighboring ghetto of Modena was implementing an innovation of far different consequences. Irritated by the longstanding frivolity and lack of moderation associated with the festivities on the night preceding the ritual circumcision, the rabbi set out to spoil a good time. In a way similar to the Catholic clergy of the Post-Tridentine Church, as Elliott Horowitz has pointed out, Aaron Berachia attempted to tone down a popular celebration by sacralizing it. In place of the frequently rowdy and obstreperous celebration, which often lasted throughout the night, the rabbi introduced the reading of the classic kabbalistic text, the *Zohar*, as the centerpiece of the festivity. This quickly transformed the joyous event into a somber occasion. By insisting on the priority of studying texts over the customary social intermingling, he succeeded, as well, in curbing female participation. And by demanding that the rite be performed by members of a ritual confraternity, he insured that only the spiritually pure and ritually fit would participate in the first place. In one sweeping declaration, the rabbi of Modena had recast a popular, secular, and undisciplined social gathering, into an elitist, solemn, structured, and deeply religious occasion. And, of course, the women stayed home.[12]

What do these four disparate scenes have in common? How might their interpretation actually lead to a more nuanced understanding of the cultural ambience of the ghetto for Jews living in the Italian cities of the sixteenth and seventeenth centuries? What can they tell us, if anything, about the contemporary meaning of ghetto and ghettoization in the Jewish experience?

For historian Robert Bonfil, the starting point for reevaluating the ghetto period is to acknowledge that it constitutes a kind of paradox in defining the nature of Jewish life and in defining the relations between Jews and Christians in Italy.[13] No doubt Jews confined to a heavily congested area surrounded by a wall shutting them off from the rest of the city, except for entrances bolted at night, were subjected to considerably more misery, impoverishment, and humiliation than before. And clearly, the result of ghettoization was the erosion of ongoing liaisons between the two communities, including intellectual ones. Nevertheless, as Benjamin Ravid has noticed, "the establishment of ghettos did not lead to the breaking off of Jewish contacts with the outside world on any level, much to the consternation of church and state alike."[14] Moreover, the ghetto provided Jews with a clearly defined place within Christian society. In other words, despite the obvious negative implications of ghettoization, there was also a positive side: the Jews were granted a legal and natural residence within the economy of Christian space. The difference between being expelled and being ghettoized is the difference between having no right to live in Christian society and that of becoming an organic albeit inferior and often beleaguered part of that society. In this sense, the ghetto with all of its negative associations could also connote a change for the better, a formal acknowledgment by Christian society, revolutionary from the perspective of previous Jewish-Christian relations, that Jews did belong in some way to their extended community.

Bonfil extends this analysis in arguing that the shift to the ghetto also constituted a radical shift in Jewish mentality. During the Renaissance, he argues, Jewish society was marked by constant migratory movement and was made up of widely scattered, miniscule, and vulnerable Jewish settlements. In this earlier period, in contrast to that of the ghetto, Jewish life was exceptionally precarious; Jews constantly felt the need to justify their continued existence before despots and democratic communes alike. They were subjected to the ugly face of Renaissance culture: Franciscan vituperations, crowd violence, even blood libels. They were merely tolerated because they offered a palliative to the poor through their money lending, performing, in Bonfil's dramatic simile, like prostitutes, a useful but despised service. Given the stark reality of Renaissance life, the high culture of the Renaissance and its new styles of thinking had little impact on Jewish cultural consciousness. Yet, with the ghettoization of Jewish life, some decades later, the patterns of Jewish culture and society were noticeably transformed. Jews were now more urbanized, more concentrated in the heart of the largest Italian cities, more polarized both economically and socially, more attuned to the sights and sounds of the Christian majority, and more secure in their new neighborhoods, despite the squalor and congestion. In the ghetto communities, Bonfil points out, the kabbalah, the mystical traditions of Judaism, performed the paradoxical function of mediating between medievalism and modernity, restructuring religious notions of space and time, separating the sacred from the secular, even serving as "an anchor in the stormy seas aroused by the collapse of medieval systems of thought," and simultaneously, "an agent of modernity." In exerting a wider impact on Jewish society through the public sermon and more popular moralistic writing, in encouraging revisions and additions to Jewish liturgy, in proposing alternative times and places for Jewish prayer and study, and in stimulating the proliferation of religious confraternities and their extra-synagogal activities, the kabbalah, in the era of the ghetto, deeply affected the way Italian Jews related both to the religious and secular spheres of their lives. In fact, the growing demarcation of the two spheres, a clear mark of the modern era, constituted the most profound change engendered by the new spirituality.[15]

Religious polarization was also accompanied by social and economic polarization. In the new urban settings, the poor became poorer while the rich became richer. And whereas the affluent had the time and leisure to pursue cultural and artistic pursuits, the knowledge of Hebrew and traditional texts among the poor conspicuously deteriorated. While rabbis complained about the loss of Hebraic literacy among the children of the ghetto, Jewish intellectuals wrote Hebrew essays, sermons, drama, and poetry using standard Baroque literary conventions. They composed complex synagogal music, as we have already seen, produced artistically elaborate synagogue interiors, ritual objects, and marriage contracts. And despite the insufferable ghetto for many, some Jews, obviously the most comfortable and most privileged, seemed to prefer their present status, as Bonfil points out.[16]

Bonfil's revisionist perspective has not yet been fully absorbed by contemporary historiography.[17] His major contribution is, no doubt, in perceiving the ghetto experience as more decisive than the Renaissance in restructuring Jewish identity. But one might still raise questions about his emphatic emphasis on the sharp rupture and discontinuity engendered by the ghetto. Did the Renaissance have no significance at all, even upon a small group of Jewish intellectuals, in the shaping of a novel and even modern Jewish cultural experience? Might one appreciate, nevertheless, certain lines of continuity between the earlier and later periods? And how might one describe the process of Jewish cultural transformation during the ghetto period? Bonfil, especially in his most recent formulation, eschews the language of influence and acculturation in defining the Jewish stance toward the majority Catholic culture, and adopts instead the more ambiguous notion of becoming aware of the Self through a "specular reflection of the Other."[18] Bonfil defines his history as one "seen from the inside," the point of view of the Jewish minority, in opposition to previous approaches that define the history of Jewish culture exclusively in terms of difference to or opposition between the Christian majority and its Jewish minority, whether minimizing or maximizing it. Bonfil maintains that these earlier approaches were responsible for the distorted picture discussed above, of seeing the Renaissance as a period of intense Jewish assimilation of the values and lifestyle of the Christian majority followed by an abrupt closure and involution of Jewish culture engendered by the ghetto system. Bonfil's "insider" perspective thus seeks to correct the distortion so as to allow the historian to place great historical significance, in terms of the formation of Jewish culture, on the ghetto period rather than the Renaissance. Leaving aside for the moment the intricacies of Bonfil's debate with the earlier historians of Italian Jewish culture, let us now return to the four scenes presented above and, following Bonfil's lead, try to interpret them in the light of his bold hypothesis, thus testing its validity, and perhaps in the process, refining it a bit more.

Simone Luzzatto's self-confidence in addressing the Doge and citizenry of Venice is surely the most dramatic example of what Mark Cohen has called "incipient Jewish attempts to reorient the Christian attitudes toward the Jews"[19] that emerged in the seventeenth century, and which include those by David de Pomis,[20] Leone Modena,[21] and Menasseh ben Israel.[22] Bonfil would surely see as paradoxical the fact that this project of influencing public opinion emerged from the ghetto. He would argue that the distancing of the ghetto actually created a proximity and new-found understanding of the other. These first steps toward presenting a rehabilitated image of the Jew before the eyes of the non-Jewish world, a kind of "anti-defamation" literature written in European languages and later translated into others, constitute a product of a modern secularism or political activism. It is rooted in an incipient psychological security stemming from the ghetto environment itself. The ghetto, in confirming the Jews' right to reside within Christian society and to belong to it, was ultimately a critical factor in providing that modicum of self-assurance that encouraged Luzzatto and the others to take pen in hand in order to demonstrate the benefits Jews offered their Christian neighbors. Luzzatto's pro-Catholic loyalties, also reflected in the writing of his Italian contemporary Modena and of Judah del Bene,[23] may have made good political sense; it might also suggest their enhanced sense of belonging to Catholic society in Italy and a deep-seated identification with its political and economic fate. As a proud citizen of the ghetto of Venice, Luzzatto believed he had every right to demand that his fellow citizens acknowledge the legal residence of Jews in their city, an entitlement the creators of the ghetto had assured.

The graduation party of Joseph Hamiz reveals another face of the ghetto ambience, its openness to scientific and medical learning. The ghetto walls could not filter out the new scientific discourse that marked the seventeenth century, the age of Galileo, Vesalius, Bacon, and Descartes. When the gates of their locked neighborhood opened at the crack of dawn, young Jewish students were on their way to the great medical schools of Italy, especially Padua. While great scientific advances often took place outside the universities, the latter still remained exciting intellectual centers, where original research was fostered and pursued, where students were regularly exposed to the latest scientific thinking even within the curricular framework of seemingly outdated medical and scientific textbooks.[24] For Jews, the encounter with the university was momentous in opening them to new vistas of knowledge, new languages, new social relationships, and even new values. The communities that sent them to study were energized by their return. The graduates often maintained social and intellectual relation-ships with each other long after graduation. More than ever before, particularly in Italy, Jewish communities were led by men who creatively fused their medical and rabbinic expertise.

The new ascendancy of the rabbi-doctor in the Italian ghetto was also the result of an emerging intellectual style marking the late sixteenth and seventeenth centuries. In the cultural ambience of the ghetto, the old synthesis between Aristotelian philosophy and Jewish revelation had been dethroned. While the old philosophy, which had arrogantly claimed to fathom the secrets of the Divine and His creation, was perceived as threatening to religious faith, the new empirical study of nature was seen as complementary and even inspirational to the faithful. With philosophy discredited within the Jewish community and disassociated from the sciences, even the most pious students of the kabbalah could appreciate the spiritual resources nature offered them. Hamiz's later infatuation with Jewish mysticism and his attempt to link it with his medical and scientific background were not so anomalous within the culture of the ghetto as they might first appear. In fact, the links between nature and spirituality were not an uncommon occurrence among Catholics as well. The growing number of rabbis flaunting their medical diplomas before their students and congregations shared a remarkable kinship with a community of Jesuit clerics, enthusiasts of science in their own right, who similarly proclaimed the majesty of God's creation before their own communities in neighborhoods just beyond the ghetto walls.[25]

Modena's recruitment of Salamone de'Rossi to compose and perform choral music in a synagogue leads us to another dimension of the ghetto ambience, not unrelated to the political and cultural apologetics of Luzzatto nor to the medical and scientific involvements of Hamiz. In all three cases, the political writer, the physician, and the composer were engaged in acts of cultural mediation between Christian and Jewish cultures, between the secular and the religious, between the old and the new. In the case of de'Rossi's music, as Dan Harrán has argued,[26] the effort was one of harmonizing differences, and again, paradoxically, of bringing Jewish and Christian cultural sensibilities under one roof in the most Jewish place of all, the synagogue. The new polyphony bespoke an awareness that what Christians think about Jews is important to the latter. Reorienting the fallacious assumptions of Christians about Judaism through an apologetic treatise was one strategy of cultural integration. Another was to transform the synagogue from an unfamiliar and offensive "cacophony of discordant sounds"[27] into a harmony of perfectly blended voices attuned to Christian ears, or at least to Jewish ones displaying a budding appreciation of Christian sensibility.

Since, from the point of view of Jewish law, only the words and the intention, not the music, should matter, the external medium could be legitimately aligned to the accepted tastes of the larger environment. Medium could never be confused with the message. And if one were to bring the music of the church into the synagogue, it had to be done in a restrained, understated, and ambiguous way, as Harrán has pointed out. The remarkable collaboration of Modena and de'Rossi in remaking the image of the synagogue through the music of the Baroque Church was not merely an audacious act, not merely a form of accommodation with the outside world, but also an integral part of that restructuring of the Jewish cultural and religious experience that the architects of the ghetto unwittingly had set in motion.

The striking cultural similarities between Jews and Christians of the Italian cities were not limited to expression of political loyalty, the study of nature and medicine, or even musical taste. As Elliott Horowitz has shown regarding the final scene presented above,[28] the Jewish religious leadership that transformed the popular celebration on the evening preceding a ritual circumcision into a subdued mystical ceremony of study and prayer, was acting in precisely the same way as the Counter-Reformation Catholic clergy. They attempted to regulate the behavior of the masses by directing their ritual and spiritual lives. They accomplished their goal by demarcating the boundaries of the sacred and the profane, by separating the sexes, and by underscoring the confraternity's central role in the ceremony to the exclusion of other willing participants. Whether or not the Jewish leaders were aware that their behavior appeared to resemble that of their Christian counterparts, it would be hard to deny that they conformed predictably and reflexively to a larger pattern associated with the Catholic Counter-Reformation.

The final scene returns us finally to Bonfil's provocative reconstruction of the culture of the ghetto. It underscores, along with the others, Bonfil's strong conclusion regarding the decisive force of the ghetto environment in restructuring ritual and liturgical norms and cultural tastes. At the same time, the four scenes point to the primary cause of these transformations. Instead of becoming more inner-directed, more independent or defiant of the norms of the majority, a greater number of Jews living in close proximity to their Christian neighbors absorbed more readily patterns of thought and behavior stemming from the Christian society that surrounded them. Their synagogues became more cathedral-like; their wedding feasts, their iconography, their entertainment, their liturgical music, their confraternal piety, their intellectual and political tastes all reflected those of the world they shared with the Christian majority. The Christian planners of the ghetto had conceived these enclosed neighborhoods as a means of leading Jews to the baptismal font. While a small number of Jews were enticed to convert, the overwhelming majority remained firmly anchored in their ancestral traditions. But in ways unbeknown to either the Christian leadership or their degraded Jewish subjects, they did succeed in remaking the Jews into a community more like them than they ever had imagined.

In a setting such as this conference, where our conversations lead us ultimately to consider the contemporary setting of the Jewish community and its challenges, it is tempting to reflect upon the ghetto experience in terms of present realities. Of course, such exercises in learning "the lessons of the past" are usually misleading and inaccurate when drawing simplistic analogies between the social and cultural world of such divergent settings as Baroque Italy and the United States at the end of the twentieth century. The "ghettos" of America, whether Jewish or otherwise, bear little resemblance to the reality we have described above. Nevertheless, we can at least rethink our image of ghettos, particularly the notion that they inevitably lead to cultural isolation and stifling parochialism. The Italian ghetto was hardly an ideal living arrangement for its Jewish inhabitants but it did provide them with two critical ingredients that ensured their survival and creativity over a long period of time: a sense of Jewish space where Jews retained a vital feeling of group solidarity and cultural autonomy; and, at the same time, a constant and intense cultural negotiation and dialogue with the outside world. The notion of open ghettos, balancing the intensity of group living with constant conversation and interaction with the larger non-Jewish society, seems to offer a paradigm worthy of some consideration in addressing contemporary dilemmas. No one would dare suggest that the horrendous conditions that created and shaped the Italian ghettos are analogous in any way to present circumstances. Nevertheless, that appealing side of their ambience should be appreciated by more than those professional students of the historical past. When understood in their complex historical settings, the Italian ghettos offer a striking blueprint of how Jewish communities survived and sometimes flourished in an often hostile and debilitating environment. In our own era, one of relative freedom and tranquility, their legacy might even provide at least some clue as to how the Jewish community might conceive of itself in facing the still formidable challenge of creative survival at the beginning of the twenty-first century.

NOTES

1.   The following represents a written version of oral comments presented informally before an audience of academics and nonacademics at the University of Scranton on March 26, 1995. I have purposely retained the informality and nonacademic quality of this presentation and also have kept my annotation to a minimum. Although presented in a different format and for a different audience, this talk draws substantially from the introduction to my edited anthology entitled *Essential Papers on Jewish Culture in Renaissance and Baroque Italy* (New York, 1992) and from my forthcoming review of Robert Bonfil's *Jewish Life in Renaissance Italy* (Berkeley and Los Angeles, 1994) to appear in a future issue of *Renaissance Quarterly*.

2.   This was not, however, the understanding of the organizer of the conference, David Myers, who opened our session by reference to the more nuanced view of Salo W. Baron in his classic essay: "Ghetto and Emancipation," *Menorah Journal* 14 (1928), 515–26.

3.   This is succinctly discussed by Benjamin Ravid in his "From Geographical Realia or Historiographical Symbol: The Odyssey of the Word Ghetto," in *Essential Papers*, 373–85.

4.   On these developments, see especially K. Stow, *Catholic Thought and Papal Jewry Policy* (New York, 1977); Idem., "The Burning of the Talmud in 1553 in the Light of Sixteenth Century Catholic Attitudes toward the Talmud," *Bibliothèque d'humanisme et Renaissance* 34 (1972), 435–59; D. Carpi, "The Expulsion of the Jews from the Papal States During the Time of Pope Pius V and the Inquisitional Trials against the Jews of Bologna [Hebrew]," *Scritti in memoria di Enzo Sereni*, eds. D. Carpi and R. Spiegel (Jerusalem, 1970), 145–65 [Also reprinted in Carpi, *Be-Tarbut ha-Renesans u-ven Homot ha-Geto* (Tel Aviv, 1989)]; D. Ruderman, "A Jewish Apologetic Treatise from Sixteenth Century Bologna," *Hebrew Union College Annual* 50 (1979), 253–76.

5.   Ravid, "From Geographical Realia," 373. See also his "The Religious, Economic and Social Background and Context of the Establishment of the Ghetti in Venice," in G. Cozzi, ed., *Gli ebrei e Venezia secoli XIV-XVIII* (Milan, 1987), 211–59; and his "New Light on the Ghetti of Venice," *Sefer Yovel le-Shlomo Simonsohn*, eds. A. Oppenheimer et al. (Tel Aviv, 1993), 149–76.

6.   K. Stow, "The Consciousness of Closure: Roman Jewry and Its *Ghet*," *Essential Papers*, 386–400.

7.   See especially, C. Roth, *The Jews in the Renaissance* (New York, 1959); Idem., *The History of the Jews in Italy* (Philadelphia, 1946); M. A. Shulvass, *The Jews in the World of the Renaissance* (Leiden, 1973; first published in Hebrew in 1955); A. Milano, *Storia degli ebrei in Italia* (Turin, 1963).

8.   R. Sennett, *Flesh and Stone: The Body and the City in Western Civilization* (New York, 1994), 212–51. Compare especially Roth's long chapter on the ghetto in his *History of the Jews in Italy*.

9.   On Luzzatto, see B. Ravid, *Economics and Toleration in Seventeenth-Century Venice: The Background and Context of the Discorso of Simone Luzzatto*. American Academy for Jewish Research Monograph Series, no. 2 (Jerusalem, 1978); The Hebrew translation of the *Discorso* (*Ma'amar al Yehudei Venezia*), by D. Lattes, with introductions by R. Bachi, and M. A. Shulvass (Jerusalem, 1950); and D. Ruderman, *Jewish Thought and Scientific Discovery in Early Modern Europe* (New Haven and London, 1995), 153–84.

10.   This is fully discussed in D. Ruderman, "The Impact of Science on Jewish Culture and Society in Venice (With Special Reference to Jewish Graduates of Padua's Medical School)," in Cozzi, *Gli ebrei e Venezia*, 417–48 and republished in *Essential Papers*, 519–53.

11.   See D. Harrán, "Tradition and Innovation in Jewish Music of the Later Renaissance," *The Journal of Musicology* 7 (1989), 107–30 [Reprinted in *Essential Papers*, 474–501].

12.   See E. Horowitz, "The Eve of the Circumcision: A Chapter in the History of Jewish Nightlife," *Journal of Social History* 23 (1989), 45–69 [Reprinted in *Essential Papers*, 554–88].

13.   See especially, "Change in Cultural Patterns of Jewish Society in Crisis: The Case of Italian Jewry at the Close of the Sixteenth Century," *Jewish History* 3 (1988), 11–30; and Idem., *Jewish Life in Renaissance Italy* (Berkeley and Los Angeles, 1994).

14.   Ravid, "From Geographical Realia," 384.

15.   This paragraph summarizes Bonfil's conclusions in the two works mentioned in note 13 above. The quotation is found in *Essential Papers*, 405. See also his "Cultura e mistica a Venezia nel Cinquecento," in Cozzi, *Gli ebrei e Venezia*, 469–506.

16.   Bonfil, "Change in the Cultural Patterns."

17.   For the time being, see H. Tirosh-Rothschild, "Jewish Culture in Renaissance Italy: A Methodological Survey," *Italia* 9 (1990), 63–96, and the reviews of Bonfil's book by T. Rabb in *Times Literary Supplement*, December 23, 1994, 25; A. Molcho in *Jewish History* 9 (1995), 113–18; by G. Mazzotta in a forthcoming issue of *Jewish Quarterly Review*; and by D. Ruderman mentioned in note 1 above.

18.   Bonfil, *Jewish Life in Renaissance Italy*, xi, 6.

19. M. Cohen, "Leone da Modena's *Riti*: A Seventeenth Century Plea for Social Tolerance of Jews," *Jewish Social Studies* 34 (1972), 287–319 [Reprinted in *Essential Papers*, 429–73; the citation is on p. 429].

20. On David de Pomis's work, see H. Friedenwald, *The Jews and Medicine* (Baltimore, 1944), vol. 1, 33–53.

21. See note 18 above.

22. See most recently the collection of essays edited by Y. Kaplan, H. Mechoulan and R. Popkin entitled *Menasseh ben Israel and his World* (Leiden, 1989).

23. On Modena's pro-Catholic loyalties, see the aforementioned article by Cohen cited in note 19; for del Bene's, see Ruderman, *Jewish Thought*, 185–98 and the earlier studies cited there.

24. See Ruderman, *Jewish Thought*, 229–55.

25. See note 9 above and Ruderman, *Jewish Thought*.

26. See note 10 above.

27. The expression is used by the French humanist François Tissard when visiting the synagogue of Ferrara at the beginning of the sixteenth century. See D. Ruderman, *The World of a Renaissance Jew* (Cincinnati, 1981), 101.

28. See note 12 above.

"THE BLESSING OF ASSIMILATION" RECONSIDERED: AN INQUIRY INTO JEWISH CULTURAL STUDIES

David N. Myers

I: *Rivers of Culture*

An eighth-century midrashic source relates that "all rivers are good and blessed and sweet and bring benefit to the world when they flow over land; but when they enter the sea, they are evil and cursed and bitter, and bring no benefit to the world."[1] The point of recalling this legend is hardly to condemn the pleasures of the sea much less to commence a discussion of Jewish oceanography. Rather, it is to provide an historical backdrop to one of the most vexing statements uttered by a Jew in modern times. Consistent with the ancient sages' charge, I have turned this statement over and over, and yet never gained more than a fleeting grasp of its meaning. And so again I submit for consideration the enigmatic words of Eduard Gans, a brilliant young German-Jewish legal historian, from 1822. Commenting on the drive of Jews in his day to break free from the shackles of insularity and particularism, Gans observed in tones strikingly reminiscent of his mentor, Hegel:

> This is the consoling lesson of history properly understood: that everything passes without perishing, and yet persists, although it has long been consigned to the past. That is why neither the Jews will perish nor Judaism dissolve; in the larger movement of the whole they will seem to have disappeared, *and yet they will live on as the river lives on in the ocean.*[2]

Separated by a vast temporal and conceptual expanse, the eighth-century midrashist and the nineteenth-century legal historian are both drawn to the metaphorical relationship between the river and the sea. For the former, the entry of the river into the ocean spells not the *disappearance* of its distinct properties but their dramatic transformation, an ontological sea change, if you will—from good to evil, sweet to bitter, indeed, from a blessing to a curse. By contrast, for Gans, the entry of the river into the sea—or more explicitly, the river of Jewish culture into the sea of European civilization—is both necessary and salutary.

But in summoning up all of our combined historical and marine biological prowess, we must ask: How precisely does a "river live on in the ocean?" Or to frame the question more generally, how do Jews avoid disappearance as a discrete group while becoming an inseparable part of a larger culture and society? This question, rife with internal tensions and contradictions, has intrigued and haunted Jews for centuries. Indeed, it has hovered above their encounter with new cultural milieux, from ancient Babylon to modern Berlin.[3] For Eduard Gans and other German-Jewish intellectuals of his day, this question consumed their daily thoughts. To a great extent, it was the same question that their parents' generation, the first generation of *Maskilim*, Jewish Enlightenment figures in Europe, had posed. And yet, the mood in the younger generation was more despairing and *Angst*-ridden over the prospect of Judaism's survival.

As children of the Enlightenment, Gans and his friends had absorbed the aspirations for emancipation and social integration that excited the passions of Moses Mendelssohn and his circle of disciples in the late eighteenth century.[4] Far more than their elders, the younger generation of intellectuals had benefitted from admission to and study at German universities, a palpable sign of progress. At university they entered a new cultural world, one in which they quickly became mesmerized by the powerful force of *Wissenschaft*—a term that conveyed, in this period, both a sense of scientific rigor and of intellectual and disciplinary unity. But the expectations of this generation, bolstered by its own experience of rapid educational advance, were abruptly and rudely challenged midway through the second decade of the nineteenth century. A powerful anti-Enlightenment sentiment swept Germany after the defeat of Napoleon, accompanied by a new wave of reaction that included anti-Jewish violence. The optimistic, at times, ebullient, spirit of the previous generation began to fade. Gans and a select circle of German-Jewish intellectuals convened in this somber atmosphere to reflect on their fate, to meditate not only on the path of Enlightenment but on their very future as Jews. This stark moment of self-reflection gave birth to the *Verein für Cultur und Wissenschaft der Juden* (Society for the Culture and Scientific Study of Jews) in Berlin in 1819.[5] Critical historical study, members of this group hoped, could both clarify the Jewish past and illumine the course of the Jewish future.

In outlining this mission, Eduard Gans, the group's president, offered his enigmatic prescription for Jewish survival. To survive, the river of Jewish culture would have to live on in the sea of European culture. Not surprisingly, this ambiguous charge was interpreted variously. Leopold Zunz, a founding member of the *Verein,* became one of the most important Jewish scholars of the nineteenth century. Throughout his long life, Zunz never surrendered his conviction that the only appropriate institutional home for Jewish studies was the German university. Consequently, he refused to accept a professorial appointment in the modern rabbinical seminaries that arose in Germany in the latter half of the century. However, Zunz was never permitted full entry into the ocean of European culture either; despite repeated entreaties, he failed to receive a position in a German university.

If Zunz marks the failure, at least in part, of Gans' vision of the river in the ocean, then Gans himself represents an ironic success. Gans too desired an appointment in a German university, though this avenue was foreclosed to him because of his Judaism. In a desperate mood, he left Germany and traveled around Europe in search of professional fulfillment.[6] After months of wandering, Gans decided to violate the first and cardinal requirement of members in the short-lived society of Jewish scholars in Berlin: in Paris in late 1825, he converted to Christianity, hopeful that this act would provide him with a "ticket of admission" to European society, as his fellow Society member, Heinrich Heine, once described his own conversion. Conversion did have the desired professional effect, earning Gans a full-time academic appointment at the University of Berlin in 1826, where he taught and wrote in the field of legal history (especially Roman law). And yet, Gans' legacy, certainly to Jewish history, is that of a *Taufjude*, literally a baptized Jew. Perhaps Gans was prognosticating his own future in his 1822 address to fellow Jewish scholars. For if anyone continued to live on as a river in a sea, it was surely the *Taufjuden.* Converted Jews in Germany tended to associate with other converted Jews or with friends and family who did not convert; moreover, despite their formal affiliation with Christianity, converted Jews often perceived themselves and were perceived by others as Jews by social and cultural affinity.[7]

The tale of Eduard Gans is interesting and powerful in its own right. But it is the larger predicament, indeed the tremulous tension, embodied in his river-sea metaphor, that extends our interest beyond the example of one German-Jewish intellectual. Gans' metaphor has often been read as an epitaph for German-Jewish culture, but I would suggest that we regard it here as an epigraph, an opening statement, for a renewed consideration of Jewish assimilation in the modern age. The term assimilation often conjures up frightful images for Jews and other minority groups, signaling the loss of collective identity to a hegemonic majority culture. But before accepting this image without comment, it might be worthwhile to revisit the career of this idea in Jewish history, particularly during the modern period. Time does not permit an exhaustive history of Jewish assimilation. However, I would like to point out the multivalence and historical complexity of the term by making recourse to a number of interesting sources drawn from Jewish history. This effort seems especially appropriate in light of recent intellectual and political trends in the United States that pose challenges to what we may call, in evocation of Salo Baron, the "lachrymose" conception of Jewish assimilation.[8] New insights drawn from the ever-malleable field of cultural studies, particularly those focused on diaspora and transnational communities, offer both novel and fertile grounds for rethinking the phenomenon of assimilation. Toward the end of this paper, we shall turn our attention to some of these new insights, taking note of their relationship to the Jewish case of diaspora identity.

But to return for a final time to Eduard Gans. If we accept that Gans captured the complexity of assimilation in his own day, we should be mindful of the fact that circumstances similar to those in which he offered his enigmatic charge have accompanied Jews in the West ever since. Indeed, nearly a century after Gans' speech, another German-Jewish intellectual pondered the prospect of Judaism's survival or, more intimately, the viability of his own existence as a Jew. This German Jew saw a number of his closest friends march to the baptismal font—not so much to advance their professional interests à la Gans, as to achieve harmony between their religious beliefs and practices, on the one hand, and between their inner spiritual world and the surrounding environment, on the other. This young intellectual, Franz Rosenzweig, found the logic of his friends compelling, and he prepared to convert to

Christianity in 1913. Rosenzweig's last act before conversion was to attend a Kol Nidre service so that he could "enter Christianity as did its founders," that is, as a Jew and not as a pagan.[9] Rosenzweig's parents, to whom he had confided his intentions, refused to attend services with him; his mother insisted that she would demand that synagogue authorities expel him as an apostate. Consequently, he found a small synagogue in Berlin populated by Eastern European immigrants.[10] As the now legendary story goes, Rosenzweig was so awed by the intensity and solemnity of the Kol Nidre service that he decided to abandon his plans to convert to Christianity and committed himself to Judaism with new passion. Over the next decade and a half, Rosenzweig, who had written little on Jewish themes prior to this time, set out to develop new theological principles to sustain Jewish identity in the modern age. These writings, and particularly his book *The Star of Redemption*, stand as one of the seminal achievements in modern Jewish thought.

Rosenzweig is interesting to us not only because he failed to consummate that which Eduard Gans had a century earlier: conversion. Nor is it even his iconoclastic *teshuvah* or return to Judaism. It is rather a certain metaphorical affinity with Gans. The title of Rosenzweig's first volume of collected essays on religious and philosophical matters, published in 1926, was *Zweistromland*, the land of two streams.[11] Curiously, there is no explicit discussion of the title in the book itself, and very little in secondary sources. But again the stream or river appears as a guiding metaphor. For Rosenzweig, the two streams in *Zweistromland* symbolized the Tigris and Euphrates, the rivers that formed the "cradle of civilization," and more germane to our concerns, that provided a rich cultural environment for the Jewish people after the destruction of the First Temple. As one interpreter, Philip Bohlman, has read Rosenzweig's title, "the Jews used the years in the *Zweistromland* of Mesopotamia (i.e., Babylonia) to enrich their culture, to absorb Persian, Greek, and Parthian influences and yet to assimilate these as their own."[12] By historical analogy, the Jews used their centuries in Europe, and particularly in Germany, to enrich their culture by integrating non-Jewish cultural sources into their own. Bohlman observes the prevalence of apparent opposites in Rosenzweig's thought and writing—first and foremost, *Deutschtum and Judentum* (Germanness and Jewishness)—and yet notes correctly that for Rosenzweig, "to be German did not negate the possibility of being Jewish."[13] What was at work was a subtle process of adaptation and reformulation not unlike the process of exegetical innovation that

Rosenzweig's critic, Gershom Scholem, once discussed in his famous essay, "Revelation and Tradition as Religious Categories in Judaism."[14]

In Rosenzweig's scheme, it is not that the river of Jewish culture is absorbed into the sea of European civilization. Rather, the river of Jewish culture runs alongside the river of European (particularly German) culture. Each has its own, rather grand existence, though together their shared properties and proximity create an enormously rich cultural plain. Rosenzweig's metaphor suggests a different under-standing of assimilation than that suggested by Eduard Gans. Assimilation does not mean absorption of a small body by a larger one. It entails a dynamic process of exchange and cross-fertilization between relative equals.

From a certain perspective, Rosenzweig's position seems short-sighted, indeed dangerously so. Was he so mired in self-delusion as to ignore the ominous signs of violence and hatred around him, even in the 1920s? Did Rosenzweig truly believe that a vibrant Judaism could take root on German soil? Did he share the deeply held view of his Jewish mentor, Hermann Cohen, that *Deutschtum* and *Judentum* were compatible? Here it would be wise to stem the tide of historical inevitability, and adopt a strategy, following Michael André Bernstein, of "sideshadowing."[15] Rather than assume that the path Rosenzweig and other German Jews were embarked on necessarily led to Auschwitz, it seems more judicious to notice the vast spectrum of Jewish expressions in the Weimar period (1918–1933), some of which advocated total immersion in German society, but many of which advocated one form or another of Jewish cultural autonomy.[16] By resisting the tendency to place German-Jewish history on a straight course leading to an inevitably tragic end, new perspectives are opened on the nature and texture of assimilation. Undeniably, there was a kind of assimilation that spelled the disappearance of Jewish identity; this version, the one stressed in the classic lachrymose conception of Jewish history, has received, and merits, a negative connotation. At the same time, there was a kind of assimilation that reflected an ongoing, dynamic, and vitalizing process of exchange. It was the cultural possibilities inherent in this process that Franz Rosenzweig and many other Jews in Weimar Germany were alive to.[17]

If the idea of two connotations for assimilation—one pejorative, the other affirmative—does not seem especially novel, it behooves me to admit that it is not. In my own reflections on the subject, I have drawn much inspiration from the late Jewish historian Gerson Cohen, who delivered a commencement address in 1966 (at the Hebrew Teachers College in Brookline) entitled "The Blessing of Assimilation in Jewish History." There is something thoroughly incongruous about this title. Why was a committed Jewish scholar and rabbi, later to become the chancellor of the Jewish Theological Seminary, extolling assimilation, no less to a group of future Jewish educators? Apart from the fact that assimilation in 1966 was a much different phenomenon than in 1996 (as evidenced by the remarkable gap in intermarriage rates in the Jewish community), Cohen sought to make the point, and quite deliberately before a group of future Jewish educators, that assimilation had an undeserved reputation in Jewish history.[18] Too often, past cultures and communities have been judged solely by their ability to survive. As an historian, Gerson Cohen was loath to pass final judgment on figures or movements from the Jewish past which did not create in Hebrew, and hence which left few visible traces of their existence in classical Jewish sources. For instance, the fact that Philo of Alexandria was virtually unknown to medieval Jews did not mean that he was irrelevant either to Alexandrian Judaism or to the broader Hellenistic society of his own day.[19]

Beyond this affirmation of the methodological imperative to contextualize (or perhaps sideshadow), Cohen proceeded to a more substantive point: namely that figures such as Philo, whose memory was not preserved in the annals of rabbinic Judaism in large measure because of their extensive contacts with non-Jewish society, were estimable, indeed authentic, Jews. The rabbis' attempts to censor them out, to insist on a static, unchanging Jewish culture, conveyed exclusively in Hebrew, were misguided. The rabbis themselves preached in Greek, and their written language was permeated with Greek words.[20] The lesson Cohen drew was that assimilation was not only a constant feature of Jewish history, but that "in a profound sense this assimilation or acculturation was even a stimulus to original thinking and expression and, consequently, a source of renewed vitality."[21] Toward the end of his lecture, Cohen echoed the distinction offered by Ahad Ha-`am, the great Hebrew essayist and Zionist, between two forms of imitation, *hikui shel hitbolelut* and *hikui shel hitharut*.[22] The first form represented total imitation of another culture to the point of self-negation. However, the second category referred to a competitive imitation in which the presence of one culture inspired creativity in another. Attraction to a great, albeit foreign, culture need not be destructive. It could also lead to empowerment, to the discovery of the distinct properties of the imitating culture.

Ahad Ha-`am pointed to the example of Jews in Egypt who "used their Greek knowledge to reveal the unique spirit of Judaism, to expose its riches to the whole world, and to diminish the genius of Greek wisdom." Gerson Cohen's own approach owes much to this conception of cultural mimesis. It was in this form of assimilation, Cohen argues, that "Ahad Ha-`am detected the signs of health and vigor rather than of attrition and decadence." Likewise, it was in this sense of the word that Cohen concluded that "assimilation properly channeled and exploited can . . . become a kind of blessing."[23]

II: *Jewishness as Hybridity*

What has been offered to this point is the genealogy of a resonant idea in Jewish history, an idea that strikes one simultaneously as banal and counter-intuitive. In its long and checkered career, assimilation has not merely had a deleterious effect; it has also vitalized Jewish culture through a ceaseless process of engagement with proximate cultures. While ensuring dynamism, it has prevented in turn the emergence of a "normative Judaism," a static, unchanging essence. Therefore, assertions of a pure and pristine Judaism should be taken with a grain of salt. This applies not only to the examples of ancient Alexandria or Muslim Spain, renowned for the high degree of cultural exchange between Jews and others. It applies as well to the supposedly insular bastion of medieval Ashkenaz, where Jews and Christians, despite their mutual hostility to the point of demonization, exchanged goods, ideas, and even ritual practices with one another.[24] Jewish culture, even in this context, was not shaped in splendid isolation; it was manifestly permeable to non-Jewish influences.

The idea that emerges then is of Jewish identity as a hybrid creation, comprised of different strands of influence. Though evident in premodern times, this hybrid quality is especially visible in the modern period, as the river metaphors of Eduard Gans and Franz Rosenzweig illustrate. Perhaps the most emblematic figure of such hybridity was Moses Mendelssohn, the great eighteenth-century savant of Berlin, whose commitments to full ritual observance of Jewish law, to a non-coercive religious tradition, and to wide-ranging philosophical study inspired a generation of Jews hungry for cultural and intellectual sustenance. Mendelssohn's example seemed to demonstrate the Enlightenment's tolerance of a new Jewish type, at once observant and enlightened, Jewish and German. And yet, few in Mendelssohn's circle of followers (least of all his children) proved capable of holding together the balance that their master had so delicately forged. Part of the reason for this was that the very tolerance promised by the Enlightenment had produced a substantially different result than Mendelssohn had hoped for. It beckoned to the Jew to enter mainstream society, while simultaneously communicating the need to constrict one's Jewishness. Thus, rather than yielding a seamless fusion of Jewish and European cultures, the Enlightenment, with its ambiguous double gesture, created a bifurcated personality, divided into national and religious, public and private, spheres.[25]

In this respect, the Enlightenment acted on the Jew in paradoxical fashion. Its terrifying "totalizing" force, so roundly condemned by a long line of thinkers from Nietzsche to Horkheimer and Adorno to Levinas to Derrida, did not produce a single, essential Jewish identity. Rather, it broke it down, fragmented it, leading at times to what Karl Marx called in his (in)famous essay "On the Jewish Question" the "decomposition of man."[26] Stated otherwise, the Enlightenment mandated the radical hybridity that marks the modern Jewish condition. Or perhaps more accurately, in a phenomenally ironic twist, we can say that it now prescribed the very fluidity that had naturally and unremarkably accompanied Jewish assimilation in previous ages.

III: *Diaspora Identities*

The impetus to undertake this reconsideration of the idea of assimilation in Jewish history does not come only from Gerson Cohen's largely forgotten lecture of 1966. Nor is it merely a function of Salo Baron's compelling argument in 1928 that political emancipation did not necessarily inaugurate a new era of resplendent progress in Jewish history.[27] Rather, it emerges in the midst of similar concerns expressed by late-twentieth-century thinkers who operate within the overlapping rubrics of cultural studies, postcolonial discourse, and postmodernism. Characteristic of this new and evolving "tradition" of writers is the exploration, and at times celebration, of hybridity as an existential condition.[28] The contributors to this new discourse include novelists such as Salman Rushdie and Toni Morrison, as well as a wide range of scholars such as Edward Said, Gayatri Spivak, bell hooks, and Homi Bhabha. Despite their diverse intellectual missions, these writers share a common interest in the interstitial, the space that exists between (and renders problematic) fixed cultural boundaries. Whether their primary focus be on the Chinese, Indians, Africans, or Caribbeans, these writers share a common language; they speak of the process of cultural formation in terms of diaspora or transnational communities.[29] Here the idea of diaspora, conveying both a sense of a native culture and of displacement from it, describes the struggle of cultural groups to stake out a position in the midst of a fast-moving current. This struggle is a political one, for dispersion invariably exposes the dispersed to the corrosive agents of hegemony and oppression. The interrelationship between dispersion and oppression, however, need not result in total submission or paralysis. In the first instance, it provides impetus to seek social and political empowerment. Moreover, it has encouraged postcolonial thinkers to examine the constructive possibilities of cultural identities that are neither native nor foreign, but dwell in "'in-between' spaces," forever resisting the stasis of a fixed identity.[30]

The connection of this new thinking about diaspora identities to the earlier discussion of Jewish assimilation should be clear by now; in the Jewish diaspora experience, assimilation has produced many varieties of hybrid identity. What is less self-evident is the reason why the Jewish case has been largely excluded from this body of writing. I would like to offer a number of brief explanations for the relative neglect of the Jewish diaspora experience, and then conclude with a number of instructive counterexamples. First, the Jewish diaspora experience has not became part of this new discourse because scholars of Jewish studies and other interested parties have been reticent to venture beyond their own intellectual province. For similar reasons, Jewish studies has not been widely integrated into the confusing and energizing debate over multiculturalism and canonicity in the American university.

But there are factors other than the disinclination of Jewish studies scholars. Perhaps more determinative is the widespread impression of scholars outside of Jewish studies that the Jewish historical and cultural experience is part and parcel of a white Eurocentric majority culture. To many, the Jews neither look different nor, in most cases, speak a different language from the majority culture. Further, both in Central and Western Europe prior to World War II and in the contemporary United States, Jews achieved a level of affluence that qualified them to be counted among the most economically privileged members of society. Conse-quently, they are viewed as not sufficiently different from, or oppressed by, the mainstream to warrant inclusion as a diaspora or transnational group, which becomes in the postcolonial lexicon an unmistakably political designation. There may be other reasons for this neglect, including the equation of Zionism with Jewishness, on one hand, and with racist imperialism, on the other.[31] It is not possible within the confines of this essay to offer a fully satisfactory analysis of these points. Nor is there sufficient time to disentangle the problematic association of Jews with the white majority culture. Even less appealing is the task of compiling a table of victimology in which the Jews, alas, would rank quite high.

It seems more important to note interesting counterexamples to the tendency to exclude or devalue the Jewish experience of diaspora. One of the most interesting sites of this countertendency, and of the new discourse of diaspora generally, is in recent black cultural criticism. Needless to say, reports of the decline of the African-American intellectual are absurdly premature.[32] Not only have figures such as Cornell West and Henry Louis Gates reinvigorated the tradition of the public intellectual in America. They have shown uncommon sensitivity to the Jewish historical experience in its creativity and in its tragedy, as well as a sincere commitment to repair fractured relations between blacks and Jews in this country. Along with their Harvard colleague, Kwame Anthony Appiah, they have questioned the essentialist (e.g., Afrocentric) currents flowing within certain academic and social circles in this country and abroad. For instance, in his important book *In My Father's House*, Appiah meticulously dissects the notion of black African *racial* purity, often used in support of political action and social segregation; he presents instead a detailed analysis of the dynamic cultural exchange that obtained between oppressor and oppressed on the African continent, and that yielded a dynamic and evolving African *cultural* identity.[33]

The affinities between this kind of model and Jewish models of cultural formation are intriguing and, in fact, have been made quite explicit in Paul Gilroy's *The Black Atlantic: Modernity and Double Consciousness*. Gilroy's book is a sustained polemic against essentialist understandings of black racial or cultural identity. A recurrent motif throughout the book is Gilroy's reliance on the homonym roots/routes to express his own clear-cut proclivities: "root" connotes a search for ultimate origins and fixed identity. By contrast, "route" conveys a sense of passage, of ceaseless and agitated movement, of dynamic creativity.[34] In celebrating the latter routes of passage, Gilroy draws direct inspiration both from the Jewish experience of diaspora and from the historical movement of Zionism. He urges a more deliberate recognition of the parallels in historical experience between blacks and Jews, both in their diaspora passages and in their respective oppressions. He also calls for acknowledgment of actual historical influences (e.g., of Zionism on early black nationalist thought).[35]

In an intriguing chapter on the great African-American leader, W. E. B. Dubois, Gilroy makes use of a familiar metaphor to summarize a central theme in one of Dubois' novelistic forays. He observes that in the conclusion of Dubois' *Dark Princess*, the union between a man and woman of different skin colors "is constructed so that the integrity of both its tributaries remains uncompromised by their confluence."[36] Although Gilroy does not relate this river-like metaphor to the writings of earlier Jewish thinkers, the predicament that it describes clearly has parallels. Indeed, it represents an idealized version of the phenomenon of "double consciousness"—a term which appears in the subtitle of Gilroy's book and which he borrows from the work of earlier black thinkers, especially Dubois.[37] Double consciousness, according to Gilroy, is the condition of women and men of African origin who act within and upon Western societies. Their experience does not entail the wholesale abandonment of a native tradition to modernity, but rather its constant and creative reformulation.[38]

What is especially commendable about Gilroy's book is the appreciation that he was not the first to articulate such an idea. Indeed, much of his book is a study of and testimony to past African-American thinkers, especially Dubois, who presciently comprehended the complicated, hybrid nature of black identity. This recognition distinguishes Gilroy from many others in the field of cultural studies, who often give the impression that they are inventing the wheel for the first time. Gilroy pushes hard to affirm the apt remark of Jean-François Lyotard that the postmodern—whatever it may be—is "undoubtedly a part of the modern."[39]

Gilroy's example is germane to our subject in two regards. First, he calls attention to a process of black cultural formation that is analogous to the process of Jewish assimilation described throughout this paper; moreover, he makes explicit the virtues of comparing the historical experiences of Jews and blacks. Such a comparative perspective can produce, as it does in Gilroy's book, a genuinely humanizing effect. Second, Gilroy chooses to position himself within a broad tradition of African diaspora history, and thereby adds an important measure of historical richness and depth to his meditations.[40]

In contemporary considerations of the Jewish community (whose leaders frequently inveigh against the evils of assimilation), it would be advisable to follow Gilroy's lead in incorporating both comparative and historical dimensions: that is, to remember first that groups other than Jews have faced similar challenges in preserving communal integrity; and second, that a measure of historical perspective can provide nuance to our understanding of assimilation. Recognizing that the problematic of assimilation is neither unique to the Jews nor unique within Jewish history is a first and important step toward comprehending the predicament of the Jewish community in the United States and throughout the world. This recognition can temper the impulse to overreact—to adopt positions that are fundamentalist, chauvinist, or in some way dismissive of the benefits of intergroup cultural exchange.

Various efforts have been made recently to articulate a vision of Jewish culture that celebrates the vitalizing potential of assimilation. The first, rather comic vision emanates from a man impersonating a writer named Philip Roth in the novel *Operation Shylock* by the author of the same name. The fictional *faux* Roth is the ideological father of a movement called "Diasporism" that "seeks to promote the dispersion of the Jews" from Israel "to those very lands (i.e., Europe) where everything once flourished."[41] A bit more serious, though not without its comic features, is the vision of an extraterritorial Jewish religious culture offered by Daniel and Jonathan Boyarin in a 1993 article in *Critical Inquiry*.[42] The Boyarins' call for a deterritorialized Judaism culminates with a curious evocation of Neturei Karta, the ultra-Orthodox and anti-Zionist sect based in Jerusalem. Far from illuminating the sort of dynamic identity–formation that the authors favor, Neturei Karta holds to a thoroughly essentialist view of Jewish identity, indeed, a kind of religious Canaanism severed both from Zionism and more conventional Jewish orthodoxy.

Both the fictional Philip Roth and the Boyarins present their respective diasporic visions *ex nihilo*, removed from the tortuous historical path of modern Jewish culture. And here, I would like to make a final point that bespeaks my own disciplinary grounding as an historian. The current cultural climate in which anxiety over group identities is expressed, be they African-American, Latino, or Jewish, has interesting historical precedents. Similar debates have occurred, for instance, in France over the course of the last thirty years, with a particularly interesting Jewish coloring.[43] In this country, attempts to balance the assimilatory impulse and the instinct to preserve group integrity long preceded the 1990s. In the second decade of this century, a group of intellectuals sought to lay the framework for a "cultural pluralism" that encouraged the free flow of ideas, customs, and habits in American society without entailing the loss of distinct group traits. Centered around the philosopher Horace Kallen, this largely Jewish circle quite naturally focused on the trials and tribulations of American Jews. Even the non-Jews in the circle, such as the writer Randolph Bourne, shared this emphasis.[44] Indeed, it was Bourne who asserted that the idea of "transnationalism," of a complex of identities that did not reside only in citizenship, was "a Jewish idea."[45] Bourne lived in an age and milieu in which the rapid currents of immigration rendered problematic "the old tight geographical groupings of nationality."[46] Navigating these currents without disappearing was an all-consuming challenge. Bourne's own instinct was to embrace "the so-called hyphenate"—the very essence of a hybrid cultural identity—for it "has actually been our salvation."[47]

It is useful to remember Bourne's discussion today, eighty years after it was published. His awareness of the tension-filled path of groups in a liberal political order anticipated both the sentiment and language of observers in our own day. At the same time, Bourne's gaze was fixed on the Jews, whose experience he believed emblematic of a much larger cultural phenomenon. Recalling Randolph Bourne can and should encourage the integration of the Jewish experience into the unfolding narrative of multicultural identity formation in the United States. In the same vein, recalling Bourne's essay, and especially the illuminating lecture by Gerson Cohen from 1966, provides the requisite historical perspective on a condition, namely assimilation, that has defined Jewish history since its inception, and will continue to vitalize and haunt Jewish communal existence well into the future.

NOTES

1. The midrash from *Pirke de-Rabbi Eliezer* is included in the monumental Bialik-Ravnitski compilation, *Sefer ha-Agadah*, revised edition (Tel Aviv, 1961), 604.

2. See Gans' second presidential address to the Verein für Cultur und Wissenschaft der Juden of April 28, 1822 in S. Rubaschoff, "Erstlinge der Entjudung. Drei Reden von Eduard Gans in 'Kulturverein,'" *Der jüdische Wille* 2 (1919). I have consulted here the English translation in Paul Mendes-Flohr and Jehuda Reinharz, eds. *The Jew in the Modern World* (New York, 1980), 192. Interestingly, though not surprisingly, the Hebrew version of Gans' speech excludes the sentence "to merge does not mean to perish." Cf.

S. Rubaschoff, "Erstlinge der Entjudung," 112, to the Hebrew translation by Rubaschoff (later Zalman Shazar) in *Ore dorot* (Jerusalem, 1971), 367.

3.   Simon Rawidowicz observes that fears of extinction have been a constant companion of Jews throughout the ages: "He who studies Jewish history will readily discover that there was hardly a generation in the Diaspora period which did not consider itself the final link in Israel's chain." Rawidowicz, "Israel: The Ever-dying People," Idem., *Studies in Jewish Thought* (Philadelphia, 1974), 211.

4.   In his important article on the Verein, Sinai Ucko refers to its members as "children of assimilation." Sinai Ucko, "Geistesgeschichtliche Grundlagen der Wissenschaft des Judentums," in Kurt Wilhelm, ed. *Wissenschaft des Judentums im deutschen Sprachbereich*, vol. 1 (Tübingen, 1967), 320.

5.   See Ucko, *passim*, and Ismar Schorsch, "Breakthrough into the Past: The *Verein für Cultur und Wissenschaft der Juden*," *Leo Baeck Institute Year Book* 33 (1988), 3–28.

6.   See Hans Günther Reissner, *Eduard Gans: Ein Leben in Vormärz* (Tübingen, 1965), 113.

7.   A curious model for this status surfaces in the 1799 proposal from David Friedländer, the Jewish Enlightenment figure, to Pastor Wilhelm Abraham Teller in which the former volunteered to convert to Christianity provided that the performance of Christian rituals not be seen as "a sign that he who performs the ceremonies is tacitly acknowledging that he accepts out of faith the dogmas of the Church." Teller rejected Friedländer's request. This letter is excerpted in Mendes-Flohr and Reinharz, *The Jew in the Modern World*, 99.

8.   The irony stems from Baron's important claim in "Ghetto and Emancipation" that the advent of modernity introduced new and vexing problems into the Jewish condition. Among the ills which Baron diagnosed is the dissolution of traditional communal bonds and, by implication, a fervent desire to assimilate. Our appropriation of the term "lachrymose conception," which Baron first used to describe the historiographical infatuation with anti-Semitism, is thus directed against the implication in Baron's essay that assimilation possesses but one connotation: a process leading to self-denial. See Baron, "Ghetto and Emancipation," *The Menorah Journal* (June 1928), 515–526.

9.   The story is related by Rosenzweig's student and close friend, Nahum N. Glatzer, in "Franz Rosenzweig: The Story of a Conversion," in Idem., *Essays in Jewish Thought* (University, Alabama, 1978), 232.

10.   See S. H. Bergmann's introduction to the Hebrew translation of Rosenzweig's essays, *Naharayim* (Jerusalem, 1960), x.

11.   Franz Rosenzweig, *Zweistromland: Kleinere Schriften zur Religion und Philosophie* (Berlin, 1926).

12. Philip V. Bohlman, *"The Land Where Two Streams Flow": Music in the German-Jewish Community of Israel* (Urbana and Chicago, 1989), xi.

13. Ibid., xii.

14. Gershom Scholem, "Revelation and Tradition as Religious Categories in Judaism," in Idem., *The Messianic Idea in Judaism* (New York, 1971), 282–303. Though this process can be characterized as dialectical, in that each culture assumes part of the other in producing a new version of itself, it is important to note that Rosenzweig had abandoned his earlier prewar interest in Hegel. While studying with Friedrich Meinecke at Freiburg, Rosenzweig produced a dissertation on Hegel and the state (published only in 1920). Following the war, however, Rosenzweig had moved away from his study of German idealism to the project of "das neue Denken," a new Jewish way of thinking. See Richard A. Cohen, *Elevations: The Height of the Good in Rosenzweig and Levinas* (Chicago, 1994), 68.

15. Michael André Bernstein, *Foregone Conclusions: Against Apocalyptic History* (Berkeley, 1994). This method allows the historical observer to imagine a number of possible occurrences or outcomes in the past rather than submit to the probability of a single occurrence that appears consistent with the trajectory of later historical events.

16. For an excellent analysis of the range of cultural possibilities, see Michael Brenner, *The Renaissance of Jewish Culture in Weimar Germany* (New Haven, 1996).

17. This is not to diminish the importance of the forces of "dissimilation," as Shulamit Volkov has formulated it, in German-Jewish culture during and after the First World War. Clearly, figures such as Rosenzweig were in retreat from the ideal of assimilation as a form of self-denial. Their search to recover a meaningful Jewish tradition reflected rejection of the older ideal, as symbolized by the *Taufjude*. For a discussion of this quest for Jewish meaning, see Steven E. Aschheim, *Brothers and Strangers: The East European Jew in German and German Jewish Consciousness, 1800–1923* (Madison, Wisc., 1982), or David N. Myers, "'Distant Relatives Happening onto the Same Inn': The Meeting of East and West as Literary Theme and Cultural Ideal," *Jewish Social Studies* 2 (1995), 75–100. Notwithstanding this quest, Rosenzweig was—by temperament, culture, and aspirations—an unmistakable product of the German cultural world.

18. According to the 1990 National Jewish Population Survey, prior to 1965, Jews married non-Jews in 9% of the cases; in 1985, the rate of marriage between Jews and non-Jews was 52%. See Barry A. Kosmin, et. al., *Highlights of the 1990 CJF National Jewish Population Survey* (New York, 1991), 14.

19. Gerson Cohen, *The Blessing of Assimilation in Jewish History*, Commencement Address/June 1966, Hebrew Teachers College, Brookline, Mass., 5–6.

20. Ibid., 5. The phenomenon of rabbis' studying and expounding in Greek is a fascinating contrast to Emmanuel Levinas' longstanding aim of translating Hebrew into Greek, by which he means Jewish thought into the universalist language of Western discourse. Levinas' ambition is a highly self-conscious one, born of an age in which Jews themselves were more familiar with "Greek" than Jewish thought. See Annette Aronowicz's introduction to Emmanuel Levinas, *Nine Talmudic Readings* (Bloomington, IN, 1990), ix–xi. I thank Bill Rowe for calling Levinas' famous "translation" project to my attention in this context.

21. Cohen, *The Blessing of Assimilation*, 7. Uriel Rappaport makes a similar point in discussing two ways of understanding the term "Hellenization" in ancient Jewish history. The first refers to a self-conscious political movement intent on adopting a "Greek way of life"; the second refers to a more incremental and unconscious process by which Hellenistic culture was absorbed into Second Temple Judaism. See Rappaport, "The Hellenization of the Hasmoneans," Menachem Mor, ed., *Studies in Jewish Civilization 2: Jewish Assimilation, Acculturation, and Accommodation* (Lanham, Maryland, 1992), 1–12.

22. See Ahad Ha-`am's classic essay, "Hikui ve-hitbolelut," in `Al parashat ha-derakhim*, vol. 1 (Berlin, 1921), 169–177.

23. Cohen, *The Blessing of Assimilation*, 9.

24. The entire question of interaction between Jews and Christians in medieval Europe has received new attention following the controversial 1993 article of Yisrael Yuval in which he argued that Jewish martyrological motifs may have been absorbed into Christian blood libels against Jews, thereby suggesting that the latter were not simply Christian inventions. See Yuval, "Ha-nakam veha-kelalah, ha-dam veha-`alilah: mi-`alilot kedoshim le-`alilot dam," *Zion* 58 (1993), 33–90.

25. Jews profoundly internalized the demand to divide their identities, as reflected in the famous Haskalah charge to be "a man in the street and a Jew at home." See Michael Stanislawski's interpretation of this line from a poem by Y. L. Gordon in *For Whom Do I Toil? Judah Leib Gordon and the Crisis of Russian Jewry* (New York, 1988), 51.

26. Karl Marx, "On the Jewish Question," *The Marx-Engels Reader*, ed. Robert C. Tucker, 33–34.

27. See Baron, "Ghetto and Emancipation," and the introduction to this volume.

28. See, for instance, Stuart Hall, "Cultural Identity and Diaspora", in Patrick Williams and Laura Chrisman, eds., *Colonial Discourse and Post-Colonial Theory* (New York, 1994), 402.

29. For a helpful survey of recent shifts in the use of the term "diaspora," see Michel Bruneau, "Espaces et territoires de diasporas," in Idem., *Diasporas* (Monpellier, 1995), 5–23. See also Gabriel Sheffer, ed., *Modern Diasporas in International Politics* (New York, 1986).

30. Homi K. Bhabha, *The Location of Culture* (London, 1994), 1. See also Paul Gilroy, *The Black Atlantic: Modernity and Double Consciousness* (Cambridge, Mass., 1993), 190.

31. Stuart Hall, for instance, explicitly rejects the notion of diaspora that refers to "those scattered tribes whose identity can only be secured in relation to some sacred homeland. . . . This is the old, the imperialising, the hegemonising, form of 'ethnicity.' We have seen the fate of the people of Palestine at the hands of this backward-looking conception of diaspora—and the complicity of the West with it." Hall, "Cultural Identity and Diaspora," 401.

32. See the March 6, 1995 edition of *The New Republic* devoted to "The Decline of the Black Intellectual," and especially Leon Wieseltier's attack on Cornell West, 31–36. Ironically, in the same month that Wieseltier's piece appeared, Robert S. Boynton devoted a long article to the reemergence of the American public intellectual in the form of African-American thinkers, noting the interesting parallels with the Jewish intellectuals of New York from a previous generation. See Boynton, "The New Intellectuals," *The Atlantic Monthly* (March 1995), 53–70.

33. K. A. Appiah, *In My Father's House: Africa in the Philosophy of Culture* (London, 1992).

34. Gilroy, *The Black Atlantic*, 19.

35. Ibid., 205–217.

36. According to Gilroy, the conclusion "offers an image of hybridity and intermixture that is especially valuable because it gives no ground to the suggestions that cultural fusion involves betrayal, loss, corruption, or dilution." Gilroy, *The Black Atlantic*, 144.

37. For Dubois, double consciousness meant that "one ever feels his twoness—an American, a Negro; two souls, two thoughts, two unreconciled strivings; two warring ideals in one dark body whose dogged strength alone keeps it from being torn asunder." This passage from Dubois' *The Souls of Black Folk* is quoted in Gilroy, *The Black Atlantic*, 126.

38. Gilroy, *The Black Atlantic*, 187–191.

39. Jean-François Lyotard, "Answering the Question: What Is Post-modernism?," in *Modernism/Postmodernism*, ed. Peter Brooker (London, 1992), 148. But cf. Gilroy, *The Black Atlantic*, 42.

40. Gilroy fails to mention in this regard the sociologist, Orlando Patterson whose 1977 book *Ethnic Chauvinism* offers interesting insights into the historical path and social status of the Jews. Patterson identifies them as a

classic "symbiotic ethnic group," who possess highly developed skills in adapting to and surviving in alien societies. Groups such as the Jews thus inhabit a "transsovereignal" plane of existence, an idea that resembles the idea of transnationalism mentioned at the end of this paper. See Orlando Patterson, *Ethnic Chaunivism: The Reactionary Impulse* (New York, 1977), 63.

41. Philip Roth, *Operation Shylook: A Confession* (New York, 1993), 44.

42. See Daniel and Jonathan Boyarin, "Diaspora: Generation and the Ground of Jewish Identity," *Critical Inquiry* 19 (Summer 1993), 693ff.

43. French-Jewish thinkers from Emmanuel Levinas to his student, Alain Finkielkraut, have generated interesting insights into the formation of Jewish identity in the Diaspora over the past half-century. Especially interesting is the attempt by Richard Marienstras and the Cercle du Gaston Crémieux to gain minority rights status for French Jews, a position that harks back to the turn-of-the-century Bundists and autonomists. See Richard Marienstras, *Être un peuple en diaspora* (Paris, 1975), 191–204. See also Judith Friedlander, *Vilna on the Seine: Jewish Intellectuals in France since 1968* (New Haven, 1990), 14–19.

44. The social ideal toward which this group hoped to move was that of a cultural "symphony," which stood in direct contrast to the guiding metaphor of the "melting pot" that so colored the immigrant experience in the United States in this period. For a fine treatment of these competing metaphors, see Moses Rischin, "The Jews and Pluralism: Toward an American Freedom Symphony," in Gladys Rosen, ed., *Jewish Life in America: Historical Perspectives* (New York, 1978).

45. Randolph S. Bourne, "The Jew and Trans-National America," *The Menorah Journal* 2 (December 1916), 280.

46. Bourne, "The Jew and Trans-National America," 279.

47. Ibid., 278.

REDEMPTION AND COMMUNITY: REFLECTIONS ON SOME EUROPEAN JEWISH INTELLECTUALS, 1900–1940

Michael L. Morgan

I n this paper I pose the question: How is the ideal of community related to social-political development and thereby to history? I address this question by examining features of European intellectual culture in the period before and after World War I. In particular, I display some stages in the "discourse of redemption" prominent in the period, in order to show how community was associated with religious, political, and even aesthetic goals and with an emerging sense of the fragmentary, discontinuous character of time and history. On the one hand, then, community was viewed as a concrete response to the alienation that riddled industrial, metropolitan life; on the other, it was perceived as a redemptive goal, a disruption in the historical process. In short, the ideal of community took its place at the intersection of history and eternity.

I. Introductory Remarks

It is natural to think of community as an historical and worldly goal. To one degree or other, communities are tangible entities. Proximate, even intimate relations do, after all, occur between individuals, and individuals are concrete, historical beings. So when we think of the establishment or recovery of community as an ideal, we tend to think of it as one toward which we might work or one that will be the outcome of the historical process. We are inclined to ask how human conduct might further the achievement of community, or perhaps whether no human action would be sufficient to bring community into being. In any case, we might reasonably think of community, it seems, as a social goal and one that is continuous with historical development.

In the early decades of the twentieth century in Europe, a tradition of discourse emerged in which the notions of community and redemption were intertwined. Many of the thinkers who employed this vocabulary had Jewish roots; some were deeply involved in Jewish life; others were assimilated and even hostile to Judaism. Some treated community as an historical goal in the sense that I have just suggested, but others, although they did think of it as a redemptive or messianic notion as well as a genuinely social one, did not conceive of it as historical in the same sense. Here I want to trace a stretch of this tradition of discourse in order to expose how this divergence occurred and what it might have meant to understand community as both a mode of redemption and as ahistorical all at once. The thinkers I shall look at are Georg Simmel, Martin Buber, Georg Lukacs, Franz Kafka, Walter Benjamin, and Franz Rosenzweig.

In a sense, exploring these figures and their thinking is also an exploration of the great cities of Europe at the turn of the century—Budapest, Prague, Vienna, Paris, but, first and foremost, Berlin. In starting with Simmel, we start with the last city, where he was born and lived most of his life. As a philosopher and a sociologist, Simmel reflected on and responded to Berlin and the momentous changes that occurred there and the other great European cities in the decades surrounding the *fin de siècle*, cultural changes wrought by rapid industrialization, new inventions and technology, increases in population, the division of labor, a flourishing capitalist consumer culture, and much else. Simmel's criticism of this era and its culture provided a foundation for the tradition we want to investigate. Buber, Lukacs, Ernst Bloch, and Siegfried Kracauer all studied with Simmel at one time or another, and his works were widely read and cited. His analysis of modern culture and its crisis became theirs, at least in part.[1]

II. Georg Simmel and the Crisis of Culture

For Simmel, the central fact about modern culture is that its development has led to three conflicts. First, between the subject's experience and objective culture; second, a conflict of expanding objective or material culture and a simultaneous tendency toward subjective internalization and isolation; and finally, an increasing estrangement of the self from the objects of material culture.[2] The very subjects responsible for the meaning of objective culture have become increasingly alienated from it. With this insight, Simmel takes his place in a tradition between Kant, Hegel, and Marx, on the one hand, and Lukacs, on the other. It is a tradition in which the overriding problem of modern culture is alienation. This insight leaves us with three questions. According to Simmel, what gives rise to this alienation and how does it affect the self? How does Simmel conceive of a genuine response to it? And finally, what implications does this issue have for the existence of community?

In *The Philosophy of Money* (1900) and his essay on the city (1903) Simmel is very explicit about the primary cause of this alienation. It results from "the growing division of labor,"[3] which, "understood in its widest sense to include the division of production, the differentiation of work processes and specialization, separates the working person from the work produced and endows the product with objective independence,"[4] and which affects the consumer in a similar way. In both cases, differentiation and a "one-sided pursuit . . . means death to the personality of the individual."[5] The unity or inner wholeness of the self is "stunted" by the fragmentation of production and by the autonomy of the product, later bought and consumed. Simmel contrasts these modalities of labor and consumption with the production of a work of art and with production in a traditional society in order to exhibit the wholeness or unity that is compromised by modernity.[6] Adopting the language of *Lebensphilosophie* and of Nietzsche, Simmel in his later essays speaks of life longing to realize wholeness: the ideal culture occurs "whenever life produces certain forms in which it expresses and realizes itself. . . .[T]hese forms encompass the flow of life and provide it with content and form, latitude and order."[7] Alienation is, at its root, the thwarting of this process.

Ultimately, Simmel may not have believed that alienation can be wholly overcome, that the crisis of culture can be resolved. At times, he suggests that the tragic moment will be superseded as culture develops.[8] At others, he praises the aesthetic dimension of individual experience, but, at best, as a momentary and temporary anticipation of the inner wholeness for which the soul yearns. At the end of "The Conflict of Modern Culture" (1911) he may have revealed his deepest and most genuine sense of resignation. Perhaps, he says, "life wishes here to obtain something which it cannot reach. It desires to transcend all forms and to appear in its naked immediacy. . . . Although this chronic conflict between form and life has become acute in many historical epochs, none but ours has revealed it so clearly as its basic theme." The end of this conflict—"absolute peace," as he calls it—"remains an eternal secret to us."[9]

For Simmel, then, the tragedy or conflict of modernity is a heightened manifestation of the characteristic tension between life and form, between subjective experience and objective culture and takes the shape of a crisis of alienation.   But does this alienation isolate individuals from each other, as it distances them from their labor, their products, their world, and ultimately from themselves?   There is evidence that Simmel thinks that it does. In "The Metropolis and Mental Life," he notices the "negative behavior" of modern subjects toward one another, and he grounds it in an attitude which he calls "reserve."[10] In the city, he claims, "we frequently do not even know by sight those who have been our neighbors for years."   Moreover, outer reserve may harbor even deeper feelings of estrangement, not only indifference but also a "slight aversion," a "mutual strangeness and repulsion."[11] To be sure, Simmel argues, this social isolation brings with it expanded personal freedom, in contrast to the restrictions of the relatively small circle of family, kin, political, and religious groups in ancient and traditional societies. But such freedom is not always valued or well-received; often it is manifest not as a feeling of comfort but rather as a sense of loneliness.[12] Alienation, for Simmel, may begin as the estrangement between the self and culture; it leads, however, both to self-estrangement and to the fragmentation of social solidarity and interpersonal intimacy.

III. Martin Buber on Unity and Community

For one semester in 1898 and then again in 1900–1901 Martin Buber studied with Simmel in Berlin.[13] It was during this same period, between 1899 and 1901, that he was also active in the *Neue Gemeinschaft*. There he lectured, among other topics, on the mysticism of Jacob Boehme, a figure whose thinking on unity and multiplicity became a central theme of Buber's dissertation for the University of Vienna entitled "Toward the History of the Problem of Individuation (Nicholas of Cusa and Jacob Boehme)" and awarded in 1904.[14] In these years Buber was immersed in a set of problems that go back to Parmenides and the pre-Socratic philosophical tradition, problems about how a plurality of individuals can emerge from an original unity and the very nature of the relation between unity and plurality. Also, in these early years of the twentieth century, Buber began to turn to the Jewish mystical tradition and especially to Hasidism. In Florence, during

1905–1906, he worked on his first two Hasidic books, one on Rabbi Nachman of Bratzlav and the other on the Baal Shem Tov, published respectively in 1906 and 1908. At the same time Buber began to collect mystical texts and testimonies from around the world; in 1909 he published a collection dealing with Chuang-Tzu and a volume called *Ecstatic Confessions*. Finally, during this same decade, Buber was actively engaged in the young Zionist movement and, in the years after 1909, he became the spiritual mentor of the community of young Zionists in Prague, the members of the Bar Kochba society.

This intense period of activity, from the turn of the century to the First World War, a period which culminated in the publication of the five dialogues called *Daniel* in 1913, "can be viewed," as Paul Mendes-Flohr has put it, "as an elaboration and refinement of [Buber's] doctrine of unity."[15] It may be an exaggeration to speak of Buber's *doctrine* of unity, but it is certainly true that in these years Buber was attracted to the idea of unity and deeply moved by the problems connected with its realization. If the problem of individuation, from antiquity to the modern period, asked how multiplicity and difference arise, then a contemporary problem of unity concerns the recovery of wholeness and unity in a world of difference and fragmentation. Unity, for Buber, expresses an ideal of wholeness and the overcoming of differentiation; as a problem, it articulates an aspiration to heal the wounds of fragmentation and alienation. It is the central concept in Buber's early writings, whatever their theme, and by focusing on it we will be able to see how redemption and community emerge as central to his work.

In *The Tales of Rabbi Nachman* Buber's conception of mysticism and ecstatic experience concentrates on the self and its relation to God. In the introduction to the volume, as he turns to Hasidism, Buber describes it as a life of "joy in God," in which "the transcendent [is brought] over into the immanent." For the Hasid, ecstasy is not escape; rather it is the soul's unfolding, an act of self-fulfilling that "flows into the Absolute."[16] The soul draws near to God by "receiv[ing] the divine" which is present in each thing. Buber's language here is impressionistic and not precise; ecstatic experience involves a unity of self with the divine, a unity articulated, on the one hand, as a movement to the divine and, on the other, as a movement of the divine within the soul.[17]

Two years later, in "Ecstasy and Confession," the introduction to *Ecstatic Confessions* (1909), Buber is more precise. Buber begins his account by pointing to everyday life and its multiplicity of feelings, perceptions, experiences, and objects. What the soul seeks is "an unknown Inward," he says, the grace of unity, an experience "beyond the commotion" of plurality, in which the soul "has submerged itself entirely in itself."[18] This experience is ecstasy, a "stepping out" that is also a turn inward. But, as Buber then claims, "in the experience of ecstasy itself there is as yet nothing that points either inward or outward." That is, ecstasy is itself an "undifferentiated experience: the experience of the I."[19] It may originate in a turn away from the multiplicity and commotion of the everyday, but it culminates in the occurrence of a unity that Buber describes as "a force, a superabundance, an infinity, in which even the most primal security, the barrier between the self and the other, has foundered." The experience of unity is a wholly uniform experience or, more precisely, a wholly uniform, totalizing event, without any limits, boundaries, or distinctiveness.

As Buber describes it, then, at the moment of ecstasy achieved there is no other, for in a sense there is no self. "What is experienced in ecstasy . . . is the unity of the I. But in order to be experienced as unity the I must have become a unity."[20] But what, then, of God? Why and in what sense is God the object of the mystic's yearning? Buber's answer is important: God and the language of God are a linguistic response to the ecstatic experience, a mythic representation that points to the ineffable event to which it responds. In *Ecstatic Confessions* he writes:

> One cannot burden the general run of occurrences with this experience; one does not dare to lay it upon his own poor I . . . ; so one hangs it on God. And what one thinks, feels and dreams about God then enters into his ecstasies, pours itself out upon them in a shower of images and sounds, and creates around the experience of unity a multiform mystery.[21]

In Judaism and Christianity, that is, the mystery of ecstasy is conceived and articulated as an enthusiastic union with the divine, as the soul's being filled with God. But in fact the language of God is not descriptive; rather it is the mystic's response, "in images, dreams, visions," to that which burns within. Ecstatic confessions are the product of this fire; they are, as Buber puts it, "a memorial for ecstasy" or a "myth" which is "the symbol of what the ecstatic has experienced."[22] God is part of the "multiform mystery" and an integral part of the conception that people have used to dignify the object of highest reverence and even aspiration; it is in this way that "ecstasy . . . became God's highest gift."[23]

For Buber, ecstasy is a response to the commotion of the everyday;

it is Buber's answer to the crisis that Simmel described. Like art, this mode of experience seeks unity and wholeness for the self. But unlike art, it achieves that goal only by reaching a unity and wholeness that is beyond the self and, indeed, beyond all things. For this reason, it is natural to wonder if ecstasy is not an asocial response to the multifaceted alienation of modern life. Is Buber here conceiving of a redemptive act that is neither historical nor communal? It is tempting to think so, until we recall that during these same years Buber was actively involved in Zionism and the movement for Jewish renewal.

Among the most revealing evidence of the intersection of his mystical interests in unity and these Jewish commitments are the famous *Drei Reden* (*Three Addresses*). The second address, delivered in Prague in 1910,[24] is entitled "Judaism and Mankind," and its central theme is the goal of Jewish life and the purpose of Judaism in the history of humankind. Within Judaism there is a profound appreciation of the dualisms that bifurcate human experience and the need to overcome that "inner duality," from which the individual cannot easily escape and "from which only redemption can liberate man."[25] The concept of the unity of God is one expression of this endeavor: "this God Himself emerged from the striving for unity. . . . The believing Jew . . . established Him as a unity above his own duality, as salvation above his own suffering."[26] Armed with this conception, the Jew "confronts mankind with the demand for unity, a unity born out of one's own duality and the redemption from it."[27] Thus, for Buber, unity is not only the goal of ecstatic experience; historically it became the goal of Jewish life and human life. The conception of God is only one of a variety of ways that this unity is expressed in life. Buber calls this idea of God a "religious synthesis" and ascribes its origin to the prophets; to Spinoza he credits an intellectual synthesis as another expression of this aspiration to unity, and to socialism a social synthesis.[28]

Here is the emergence of the communal dimension of the redemptive. Judaism "proclaims a world in which dualism will be abolished, a world of God which needs to be realized in both the life of the individual man and the life of the community."[29] Here the fire that burns in the mystic becomes a mandate to bring unity to the world, in diverse settings and hence in diverse ways. These include the interpersonal setting and the way of a just and benevolent society:

It is this striving for unity that has made the Jew creative. . . .
Striving to evolve unity out of the division of the human

community, he conceived the idea of universal justice. . . .
Striving to evolve unity out of the division of the world, he
created the Messianic ideal, which later, again under the
guiding participation of Jews, was reduced in scope, made
finite, and called socialism.[30]

Buber has found a way to bridge the gap between the seemingly a-
historical mystical experience of unity and the very historical experience
of Jews in the world. The experience of unity may occur at an instant,
in a moment of eternity as it were, but the creation of genuine
community occurs in time. Ecstatic experience is only the origin of
redemption from duality and "the commotion of the everyday." Its
sequel lies in the striving and realization of unity in life, a process that
is as historical as the transcendent experience is eternal.

IV. Georg Lukacs: Soul, Form, and Life

Georg Lukacs was among those who praised Buber's mysticism.[31]
The story of Lukacs' early life and work, prior to and including his
conversion to Bolshevism in 1918, is not an uncomplicated one.[32] But
it does have a well-defined core. Lukacs inherits from Simmel and Max
Weber a sense of the crisis of modern culture; he seeks to articulate "a
precise conceptual diagnosis of this 'crisis'" and then to find a way out
of it, "or at least to find norms offering a guide to right conduct within
it."[33] His chosen venue for dealing with these issues is philosophical-
literary analysis; his responses are aesthetic and increasingly ethical, but
colored at times with a respect for mysticism.

Born into a totally assimilated and indifferent Jewish family in
Budapest, from a young age Lukacs took a deep interest in drama and
literature.[34] In 1904, at age 19, he helped found a progressive repertory
company in Budapest, the Thalia Society, for which he played an
administrative role for four years. From 1906 to 1907 Lukacs was in
Berlin, studying with Simmel, when he was notified by a friend of a
competition in Budapest for a work of literary criticism. He set out to
employ Simmel's appreciation for the social context of art in writing a
history of modern drama, which won the Kristina Lukacs Prize and
launched his literary career.[35] All of this—Lukacs' profound interest in
literature, the influence of Simmel, and his appreciation for the social
and historical context of art—provides the background for Lukacs' first
book, a collection of essays, entitled *Soul and Form*. Many of the essays
were first published in the journal *Nguyat* in 1908 to 1910, then

collected and published in Budapest in 1910, and subsequently translated and republished in an expanded edition in Germany in 1911. *Soul and Form* contains, in its German edition, an introductory piece on the nature of the essay and nine essays, each on a different author and each exploring artistic alienation and the tragedy of culture.[36]   Of special interest to us are the essays on Kierkegaard and on Paul Ernst, a playwright and close friend of Simmel's.[37]

The basic concepts of the essays, brilliantly discussed by Gyorgy Markus, are life, soul, and form, and the central question which the essays address is whether soul can bring form to life, thereby overcoming alienation and achieving authenticity and redemption. Lukacs' answer to this question, drawn out of these several episodes of philosophical-literary analysis, is that soul, especially the soul of the artist, cannot succeed; authenticity is impossible. That is the tragedy of culture for art and the soul, namely that "it seeks to build a crystal palace out of air, to forge realities from the insubstantial possibilities of the soul,"[38]   but cannot succeed.

In his essay on Kierkegaard, which Buber read and about which they corresponded,[39] Lukacs takes form to be "the only way of expressing the absolute in life;"[40] it is that which brings value and meaning to the everyday world. To accomplish this requires a gesture, the act of bringing form to life, or of trying to do so. But, Lukacs asks, can the gesture succeed? "Can there really be a gesture *vis-à-vis* life?"[41] In his own life, Kierkegaard's gesture was the breaking of his engagement to Regine Olsen, his "leap by which [his soul] leaves the always relative facts of reality to reach the eternal certainty of forms." It was the act whereby Kierkegaard sought to abandon the love of Olsen on behalf of the unconditional and absolute love of God. Because he loved her, he had to leave her, to leave the relative in order to attain the absolute.[42] "Regine Olsen was for Kierkegaard no more than a step on the way that leads to the icy temple of nothing-but-the-love-of-God."[43] But this temple, so to speak, is not in the world nor in life; life cannot by its very nature bear the unconditional and absolute. Kierkegaard's "tragedy was that he wanted to live what cannot be lived."[44] What he sought was an unconditional love in life in order to give meaning to life as he lived it. But, as Lukacs claims, this is impossible. In Simmel's terms, redemption requires the impossible, an objective culture that expresses accurately and authentically the self, an objective culture that constitutes a genuine unity with the subjectivity of the self. Hence, what Kierkegaard came to realize is the inescapability of the tragedy of culture.

These themes reach a heightened pitch in Lukacs' most famous essay in the collection. The essay on Paul Ernst, "The Metaphysics of Tragedy," was added to the German edition after its publication in the first issue of *A Szellem*, a short-lived journal edited by Lukacs and his friend Lajos Fulep in 1911.[45] Tragic drama represents what Lukacs described in the Kierkegaard essay as the tragedy of "real life," the tragedy of the miracle that bursts into life and seeks (although it fails and, Lukacs believes, must fail) to make that life clear, unambiguous, and fulfilled.[46] The miracle is a "revelation of God;" it is the event of form striving to bring order and meaning to life, ultimately without success. Tragic drama is the picture of this unfulfilled event, the failure to realize perfect selfhood. It tries to portray the timeless in time, to express a mystical experience in human language, and hence it is, in a sense, paradoxical.[47]

To be sure, the tragic experience of the self and the mystical experience are only similar and not identical. Mystical experience involves a merging of the self within a supreme, unqualified unity; tragic experience has its essence in selfhood and the force of selfhood. Nonetheless, for Lukacs, the two experiences are deeply similar, and both are conflicted. Dramatic tragedy is their common expression. It "is the form of the high points of existence" and of a selfhood that is too much for reality to bear.[48] It is the literary representation of a metaphysical failure and hence of the permanence of alienation and the crisis of culture as Simmel saw them. There is a tone of pessimism in these essays or at least a tone of resignation, for even art cannot succeed in its task. Art can aspire to bring meaning to human existence, and it can grasp the ground of that meaning. But in the end it must fail, for "real life" or fulfilled selfhood cannot be realized in history and in the world. Alienation is our inescapable destiny; redemption is impossible.

In the second and final issue of *A Szellem*, in December of 1911, Lukacs published a tremendously important, if enigmatic, piece entitled "On Poverty of Spirit." It is a dialogue that reveals a major change in Lukacs' thinking and in his general attitude. It unveils what Lee Congdon has called "a turn from tragedy to utopia."[49] The essays of *Soul and Form* were written under the shadow of Lukacs' own "tragic" relationship with Irma Seidler, a young artist whom he had met in December of 1907. During 1908 their relationship became intense, and as it did, so did Lukacs' conviction that closeness to another person was incompatible with his own creativity and his own work. Irma came to represent for Lukacs what Regine Olsen did for Kierkegaard: the life and love that could not be reconciled with transcendent desire.[50] By the end of the year, they had separated. Increasingly, in 1908 and thereafter, Lukacs came to feel the inevitability of alienation and loneliness, and the essays of *Soul and Form* reflect this sense of resignation, that soul and life could not be united. This sense was present as the relationship with Irma Seidler was deteriorating. In a letter of November 1908 that was never sent, Lukacs speaks of his sense of "complete loneliness, of total exclusion from all human community," and of Irma's desire "to redeem him." But she failed, and he asks whether it is not his fate always to lose out when he tries to establish person to person relationships. "Goodness," he says, "has left me forever."[51]

On May 18, 1911, Irma Seidler committed suicide. During November, riddled by the guilt of having abandoned her and having been fated to do so, Lukacs contemplated suicide. The crisis passed, however, and, as Congdon notes, he came to see how alienation could be overcome and redemption could occur. This insight he displayed in the crucial piece "On Poverty of Spirit."[52]

The framework of the dialogue is autobiographical: Martha, whose sister had recently committed suicide, is reporting to an unnamed woman her conversation with her sister's lover, that woman's son, after the suicide. The lover, Lukacs himself, acknowledges guilt for his lover's death; he heard her cry, he says, and yet could not respond. Only Goodness—his term in the piece for the absolute ground of meaning—could have given him real insight, but Goodness is a miracle, an act of grace, divine. One cannot bring it about; it must be given. As Lukacs puts it, Goodness is "salvation," "man's true discovery of his home," but one does not create it or construct it.[53] All of this revealed to Lukacs the deep error of his life's work; he had hoped to gain access to the absolute, to grasp it and bring it into life. But this is mistaken; Goodness must be received and not created; beyond ethics lies religion. And so Lukacs reconceives, in the dialogue, a new strategy for his life; the authentic life is one that prepares the self to receive redemption, to be saved. It is to achieve, in the mystical sense, the "poverty of spirit," "liberating myself from my psychological limitations" in order to prepare the self for virtue, which is not something we have but is something which comes to possess us.[54]

In the dialogue, Lukacs comes to realize the inauthenticity of his old aspirations; an authentic life seeks to transform the mundane in order to receive Goodness as a gift of grace. Authentic life is not an escape into the otherworldly or the spiritual. Rather, it involves a recognition of the needs of this world in order to welcome salvation and to overcome alienation and estrangement. The alienation is twofold, the self from the other and the self from itself. Virtue is both wholeness of self and community with others. The old ethics of duty had led Lukacs to sacrifice his beloved for his work; the new ethic of virtue will lead to a unity between work and the everyday, between the self and the other, but it is a unity conceived as utopian, a goal for which we can prepare but which is not wholly ours to achieve.[55]

The life of virtue, graced by Goodness, appears in "On Poverty of Spirit" as the manifestation of perfect unity and hence community, but it is not a historical goal. It is a messianic hope. One can prepare for it, but there is no reason to think that history is moving toward it. By 1915, after Lukacs had moved to Heidelberg and become a favored member of the Max Weber Circle, and after the outbreak of the war, which he opposed with passionate intensity, the historicity of this goal impressed itself upon Lukacs. The literary expression of this conviction, that history itself is moving toward an ideal community in which authentic selfhood will be realized, is *The Theory of the Novel*. Originally intended as the introduction to a book on Dostoyevsky, the book sets out a philosophy of history based on the interrelationships of literary genre and social form. In the final paragraphs, Lukacs acknowledges in Dostoyevsky the prophet of redemption. In his work there emerges the portrait of a new, unified, organic community, an anticipation of a world yet to be realized. With this work a new element of messianic but historically grounded optimism, in the face of threatening and horrific realities, enters Lukacs' thinking.

V. The Fragmented World of Franz Kafka

In these same years, however, both before and after the war, this optimism was far from universal. Surely Franz Kafka did not feel it.[56] By 1908 Kafka had received his law degree at the German University in Prague. He had settled into what would become a life-long association with the Workers' Accident Insurance Institute for the Kingdom of Bohemia in Prague and had written his earliest stories, eventually collected in a small volume published in August of 1912 (*Betrachtung, Meditation*). About that time as well, Kafka first met Felice Bauer at Max Brod's house and shortly thereafter began his long, tortuous relationship with her. During the night of September 23–24, he wrote his first major story, "The Judgment," a document, like Lukacs' "On Poverty of Spirit," which was both autobiographical and momentous.[57]

Kafka's writings defy abstraction in favor of a bleak, gripping concreteness. They and his life mingle in a drama of despair and suffering. His life and his writing portray the same phenomenon, of a self in conflict—with his father, his family, women, the everyday life of bureaucratic employment, his body and its health, with himself and his writing, and with Judaism and its God. Simmel analyzed modernity to uncover its critical tensions; Kafka does not analyze in any normal sense, nor does he theorize. He experiences and dramatizes the torment of those experiences. He does not write about living amid the cultural crisis, which Lukacs also acknowledged; rather, he writes that crisis and lives the crisis by writing it.

In "The Judgment" Kafka is its chief character, Georg Bendemann, writing a letter to his friend in Russia about his recent engagement. The letter completed, Georg, enters his father's dark bedroom and has an almost surrealistic encounter with his father in which he is bombarded by accusations, exposed and dominated, until finally he submits to the judgment against him. But why submit? Why jump to his death? Because he has chosen the engagement to his fiancée over the well-being of his friend in Russia, and for Kafka, as for Lukacs, Russia represents art, creativity, literature. Georg has chosen life over writing, and ironically it is his father who charges him for his failure and who utters the judgment against him. He must die; "the decision to marry becomes inescapable at the same time that it becomes worthless,"[58] or perhaps more than worthless. "The Judgment" is about the tension between art and the prosaic, between Kafka's daily labor at the insurance institute, at which he excelled and yet which he often bemoaned, and his nightly devotions to writing, between his yearning for marriage, family, and love and his phobic resistance to them. In short, "The Judgment" probes the very conflict that Lukacs had felt toward Irma Seidler and the gesture that Lukacs took Kierkegaard to have made; it explores the passion for transcendence as it strains against life, the yearning for love, and personal relationship.

Kafka's torment is present in his writing everywhere—in his stories, his diaries, and his letters; it is also present in his Jewish personae.[59] "Assimilated Jew, anti-Jewish Jew, anti-Zionist, Zionist, believer, atheist —Kafka was indeed all of these at different times in his development, sometimes all at once."[60] As he famously recounts, in his letter to his father of 1918, Kafka took his Jewish world in Prague to be arid and worthless, if not also hypocritical.[61] His friends' Zionist passion did not resonate in him, and only late in life did he turn to Zionism.

Yet Kafka was drawn to Judaism in complicated ways. He was attracted to the Yiddish theater troupe that performed in Prague at the Café Savoy in May of 1910, and when a different troupe returned in October of 1911, Kafka attended their performances devotedly and befriended their leader, Yitzchak Löwy.[62] In this mode of theater Kafka seemed to find a kind of wholeness, a unity of actors and audience, of artist and Jew, that signaled possibilities from which he felt so estranged.[63] Here Kafka took up a view that was not uncommon among Western European Jews: "humble and proud, endowed with an exuberant life that did not contaminate his purity, the Eastern Jew . . . was everything the Western Jew lost by trying to become civilized."[64] In the Eastern Jew and in particular in Lowy, Kafka saw beyond his own alienated, conflicted Judaism. But what he saw was not theology or doctrine; it was "not faith so much as a living community."[65]

And there is evidence that at a later time Kafka felt himself a part of that search for such community, if not a part of its realization. To some readers, for example, "A Report to an Academy," first published in Buber's journal *Der Jude* in 1917, represents Kafka's acknowledgment of the pathos of assimilation,[66] while "The Great Wall of China," also published in 1917, expresses what a Judaism means that is remote from its orienting center and its historic past and yet is able to preserve a sense of community.[67] If the story of Kafka's conflicted Judaism is one dimension of his struggle for wholeness and redemption, perhaps, unlike other dimensions, it reflects some measure of reconciliation.

Both Buber and Franz Rosenzweig were to revere Kafka's *The Castle* as the most brilliant portrait we have of human life in a world cut off from the divine.[68] Might it be just as true to speak of his writings—all of them, the stories, the diaries, and the letters—as a remarkable record of estrangement of all kinds? If so, Kafka's writing may not reveal any hope for us; it may instead testify to the fractured world of early twentieth–century industrial, urban, disenchanted society, to a world without truth, without an absolute, without redemption.

Walter Benjamin seems to have believed something like this of Kafka. In an important letter to his friend Gershom Scholem, Benjamin wrote:

> Kafka's work presents a sickness of tradition. Wisdom has sometimes been defined as the epic side of truth. Such a

definition stamps wisdom as inherent in tradition; it is truth in its haggadic consistency. It is this consistency of truth that has been lost. Kafka was far from being the first to face this situation. Many had accommodated themselves to it, clinging to truth or whatever they happened to regard as truth and, with a more or less heavy heart, forgoing its transmissibility. Kafka's real genius was that he tried something entirely new: he sacrificed truth for the sake of clinging to its transmissibility, its haggadic element. Kafka's writings are by their nature parables. But it is their misery and their beauty that they had to become *more* than parables. They do not modestly lie at the feet of the doctrine, as the Haggadah lies at the feet of the Halakah.[69]

For Benjamin, Kafka's writings are marked by striking brilliance and beauty, but they are also marked by sickness and misery, "the purity and beauty of a failure,"[70] of a cosmic emptiness that remains unfilled. Whatever Benjamin thinks of Kafka's real achievement, he is clear about the situation which his writings portray, a world radically alienated from the absolute, from meaning and purpose.[71]

VI. Walter Benjamin, Redemption, and History

In Benjamin's reading, figures such as Buber, Lukacs, and Rosenzweig also faced this situation of the loss of truth and its consistency, but unlike Kafka, they clung to what they took to be truth and accepted in some sense its incommunicability. Mystical experience and the cult of experience was no more to Benjamin's liking than it was to Kafka's, although he was drawn both to a variety of forms of experience and to mystical cosmology and metaphysics. Yet Benjamin thought that it was not experience but rather criticism—philosophical, literary, and cultural—that could have some redemptive effect. In Simmel's terms, the crisis of culture could be confronted; some measure of salvation could be realized. The question is, how?

In order to answer this question we need to consider one strand of Benjamin's very difficult thinking, the messianic strand.[72] Benjamin's association with the German youth movement, and its spiritual goals, shaped his commitment to messianism in the prewar years. It was galvanized on August 8, 1914, when his closest friend, the young poet Paul Heinle, and Rivka Seligson, the sister of his friend Carla, in despair over the war, took their lives in a suicide pact at the Meeting House of

the Berlin youth movement, which Benjamin had helped to found. Later
Benjamin would recall those days as "an heroic attempt to change the
attitudes of people without challenging the structure of society itself."
But it was an attempt that failed.[73]

One of the outcomes of the crisis, for Benjamin, was the realization
that history and the messianic moment, time and eternity, are
discontinuous. To be sure, this realization is one that takes shape over
a number of years, but by 1920 it is in place. The key document that
testifies to it is a short, two-page piece, discovered among Benjamin's
unpublished papers and dated 1938 by Adorno but 1920–1921 by
Scholem.[74] In the "Theologico-Political Fragment," as Adorno titled it,
"Benjamin denies any direct connection between secular political action
and the intervention of a messianic nature into history."[75] In Benjamin's
own words, "nothing historical can relate itself on its own account to
anything Messianic."[76] Theocracy, he says, is a religious and not a
political idea. Eternity is not an historical category; rather it redeems
history by ending it and introducing an utterly distinct domain. By the
early 1920s, then, Benjamin had come to separate redemption or
messianism from history, politics, and everyday human action. In this
regard, he had broken with Lukacs and with those like Hegel who
associate freedom and rationality with activity and political self-
determination and who take redemption to be the goal of history. For
him, as for Kierkegaard, redemption comes at any moment, as an act of
grace. The Messiah can enter time through any instant, suddenly and,
with respect to history, catastrophically.[77]

In the years after 1927, these reflections on history and eternity form
the background for a conception of literary and cultural criticism that
prepares for such a Messianic moment. This literary and cultural
criticism is, in a sense, a revolutionary activity, grounded in a mystical
theory of language, nourished by a deep appropriation of romantic
literary theory and various strands of modernism, and wedded to a
catastrophic view of history. As Michael Jennings puts it, for Benjamin
"critique [is] the isolation and redemption of truth."[78] Critique examines
relics of the past to free or redeem them from their "mythic, debased
context," and at the same time the present too is redeemed, as it comes
to recognize "itself as prefigured in that past image and only thus
discovers its true nature."[79] What critique generates, through a kind of
cognitive "collision of static images," is an "astonishment that leads us
to reflect upon our historical condition and that eventually leads to the

erasure of the condition of oppression."[80] Or, at least, it gives rise to an astonishment that *can* lead to such redemption.

As Jennings, among others, points out, "redemption" is a central notion for Benjamin throughout his career.[81] It emerges early in his writings on the youth movement and then in his thesis on the romantics; it resurfaces in his encounter with the surrealists and with Proust and flourishes after 1924 as Benjamin appropriates themes from Brecht and Marxist thought.[82] But it is a complex, multivalent notion.

Redemption has many objects, so to speak, and several stages or modalities. First, the past is redeemed, when a "destructive" analysis breaks through the false, obscuring totalities, narratives, or myths, as Benjamin calls them, and wrenches a text or cultural object from its mystifying context in order to bring its truth to clarity.[83] Second, the present is redeemed, when its truth is disclosed as it is recognized as prefigured or anticipated in those images of the past. Third, the critic's understanding is redeemed, when he or she achieves a clarified intuition of the truth about the world as it is revealed in the dialectical images of past and present. And finally, the world itself is redeemed, when that new understanding, arising out of the explosive conflict of images, generates an "astonishment" that itself leads to action in behalf of the oppressed, a liberating or redeeming action.[84] Moreover, if there are several objects of redemption for Benjamin, at least in his latest thinking, then there also seem to be several modes of redemption—from literary and cultural critique to cognitive revision and finally to engaged action.[85]

Benjamin expresses these goals and convictions nowhere better than in his notes for the Arcades Project and in his aphorisms "On the Concept of History." There he ties past to present with the expectation of redemption and acknowledges "in every generation" what he calls a "*weak* Messianic power."[86] Every present generation, that is, has the capacity to rip the present, oppressive, and corrupt world out of history and to bring to it what Rosenzweig called "eternity," "to interrupt the course of human events and, ideally, bring human history to an end."[87] A genuine critical engagement with the past is not disinterested; nor does it enslave itself to a causal map or some other explanatory pattern.[88] Instead, it takes an interest in certain moments or eras of the past and seeks "a tiger's leap into the past,"[89] the discovery of images that expose present truth "at a moment of danger," when, as he puts it, "both the content of the tradition and its receivers" live with the "threat . . . of becoming a tool of the ruling class," with the threat of "barbarism" and of oppression.[90] Indeed, Benjamin makes it clear that redemption is both apocalyptic and social: "the awareness that they are about to make the continuum of history explode is characteristic of the revolutionary classes at the moment of their action."[91] This is what he later calls "a revolutionary chance in the fight for the oppressed past,"[92] which is both a past bound by or oppressed by a narrative and a past that discloses the truth about oppression.[93] But if redemption is social, it is not political, as several commentators have argued, and hence it has no determinate content.[94] As Jürgen Habermas has put it, in his influential essay "Walter Benjamin: Consciousness-Raising or Rescuing Critique," "a critique that sets out to rescue semantic potential with a leap into past *Jetztzeiten* has a highly mediated position relative to political praxis. On this, Benjamin did not manage to achieve sufficient clarity."[95]

In the end, then, for Benjamin, the critical encounter with objects of art and culture may be as far as redemption can extend. Perhaps, even if "profane illumination" is not a political deed, as Habermas reminds us, it is for Benjamin as redemptive as we can expect.[96] But, even if redemption is conceived as disruptive and a-historical in one sense, it need not be restricted to a kind of insight. There may be more to redemption than a purified mode of understanding. Certainly Franz Rosenzweig thought that there was.

VII. Franz Rosenzweig on Redemption and History

Benjamin was first introduced to Rosenzweig's *The Star of Redemption* in 1921, shortly after its publication, by Scholem, and there is reason to think that Benjamin had great respect for the work. He refers to it several times, and similarities of theme and concept can be found between Rosenzweig's *Star* and Benjamin's final aphorisms on history. Like Benjamin, Rosenzweig was moved by the catastrophic nature of the war and by a despair over modernity and the estrangement and excessive rationalism that came with it.[97] To Rosenzweig, eternity was the ideal of history, but, like Benjamin, he believed that it would come as an interruption, oblique to historical experience and narrative history. Hence, for Rosenzweig, there is something exemplary about Jewish life and its ritual vehicles for prefiguring redemption; these special moments of Jewish life and the Messianic redemption are discontinuous with everyday, historical experience.[98] There are, then, similarities between the two, but there are also differences, more than Rosenzweig's special interest in Judaism and Jewish life. What is missing, or at least uncertain, in Benjamin is present in Rosenzweig, namely, a sense for the communal dimension of eternity and hence of redemption.

According to Rosenzweig, "all the phases of [Jewish] history are simultaneous;"[99] the essence of Judaism is eternity, and in a way Jewish life must always focus on that eternity. This is Rosenzweig's way of saying that any moment of Jewish life can be a venue for eternity, for redemption; the Messiah can interrupt history at any instant. And when he does, in anticipation of the final redemption, as a glimpse of eternity itself, redemption comes to Jews as a community of a special kind. In Part Three of *The Star* Rosenzweig says or suggests just this: What testifies to the eternity of the Jewish people is the people's rootedness in itself. And this rootedness in itself "means no more and no less than that one people, though it is only *one* people, claims to contain the Whole. . . . With reference to the Jewish people this means that it would have to collect within itself the elements of God, world, and man of which the Whole consists."[100] In short, the Jewish people is a unique kind of community, an inclusive community whose ritual and social life seeks greater and greater wholeness and greater and greater unity. Rosenzweig moves with restraint toward an account of that community until, as he prepares to discuss the Days of Awe, he draws close to a description. This is a community, he says, on "the way to the all-embracing common unity where everyone knows everyone else and greets him wordlessly—face-to-face."[101]

With Rosenzweig's insight, I close these reflections. With his thinking, community as a redemptive moment is both social and yet eternal; his thinking blends elements from other thinkers—the prominence of alienation and fragmentation, the ideal of community, and the tragedy of culture that infects history as it is—with a sense of the disruptive nature of messianism that we find in Benjamin. I have tried to show how, in the thinking of several European Jewish intellectuals of the early part of the century, there develops a tradition of discourse in which several notions are clustered—redemption, the crisis of modern culture, alienation, community, unity, history, messianism. This tradition plots a movement from a deeply ahistorical ecstatic experience of unity to a social conception of community. It then shows how that communal goal resonates with the notions of history and eternity. These themes provide an important context within which to discuss the thought of these thinkers and that of many others of this period. Moreover, this tradition of discourse has emerged, in various ways, in more recent Jewish thinking in the second half of this century. To be sure, the specter of the Holocaust and developments in postwar culture have modified the way in which this tradition has been received in the past several decades and how it has influenced recent thinking. But, I would argue, it is a tradition that is nonetheless present to this day.

NOTES

1.   See Lukacs's comment quoted by Lawrence A. Scaff, "Georg Simmel's Theory of Culture," in *Georg Simmel and Contemporary Sociology*, eds. Michael Kaern, Bernard S. Phillips and Robert S. Cohen (Dordrecht, 1990), 283.

2.   See Scaff, 284–85; Deena Weinstein and Michael A. Weinstein, "Dimensions of Conflict: Georg Simmel on Modern Life," in *Georg Simmel and Contemporary Sociology*, 346–47; Georg Simmel, *The Philosophy of Money*, second ed. (London, 1990), 448–50; Kurt H. Wolff, ed. *The Sociology of Georg Simmel* (New York, 1950), 409–24. On Simmel, see David Frisby, *Fragments of Modernity: Theories of Modernity in the Work of Simmel, Kracauer and Benjamin* (London, 1988), Idem., *Sociological Impressionism: A Reassessment of Georg Simmel's Social Theory* (London, 1992); Wolff, *Georg Simmel 1958–1918* (Columbus, 1959).

3.   Simmel, *The Philosophy of Money*, 63; Wolff, *The Sociology of Georg Simmel*, 422–24.

4.   Simmel, *The Philosophy of Money*, 457.

5.   Wolff, *The Sociology of Georg Simmel*, 422.

6.   Cf. Scaff, 288.

7.   Simmel, *The Conflict in Modern Culture and Other Essays* (New York, 1968), 11, 148.

8.   Scaff, 290–91; Simmel, *The Conflict in Modern Culture*.

9.   Simmel, *The Conflict of Modern Culture*, 25.

10.   Wolff, *The Sociology of Georg Simmel*, 415.

11.   Ibid., 415–16.

12.   Ibid., 418.

13.   On the early Buber, see especially Maurice Friedmann, *Martin Buber's Life and Work: The Early Years 1878–1923* (New York, 1981); most important of all is Paul Mendes-Flohr, *From Mysticism to Dialogue: Martin Buber's Transformation of German Social Thought* (Detroit, 1989) and his introduction to Martin Buber, *Ecstatic Confessions: The Heart of Mysticism* (San Francisco, 1985).

14.   See Friedman, 77–85; cf. Mendes-Flohr, 54–57.

15.   Mendes-Flohr, 63.

16. Buber, *The Tales of Rabbi Nachman* (New York, 1956), 10.

17. Ibid., 10–17.

18. Buber, *Ecstatic Confessions*, 1–2.

19. Ibid., 4.

20. Ibid., 5.

21. Ibid., 4.

22. Ibid., 10.

23. Ibid., 3.

24. In addition to the second of the "Three Addresses" in Buber, *On Judaism* (New York, 1967), one might also look at the essay "The Teaching of the Tao," reprinted in Buber, *Pointing the Way* (New York, 1957), 31–58.

25. Buber, *On Judaism*, 27.

26. Ibid., 27.

27. Ibid., 32.

28. Ibid., 32.

29. Ibid., 33. Compare ibid., 27: "A striving for unity: for unity within individual man; for unity within divisions of the nation, and between nations; for unity between mankind and every living thing; and for unity between God and the world."

30. Ibid., 28.

31. See note 45 for reference to Lukacs' review of Buber's two Hasidic books.

32. There are some excellent accounts. See Georg Lukacs, *Record of a Life: An Autobiographical Sketch* (London, 1983); Lee Congdon, *The Young Lukacs* (Chapel Hill, 1983); Mary Gluck, *Georg Lukacs and His Generation 1900–1918* (Cambridge, 1985); Agnes Heller, "Georg Lukacs and Irma Seidler," in Heller, ed, *Lukacs Reappraised* (New York, 1983), 27–62; and, in the same anthology, Gyorgy Markus, "Life and Soul: The Young Lukacs and the Problem of Culture," 1–26. It is very clear that others saw the young Lukacs as having religious or quasi-religious interests; I am thinking of Marianne Weber's oft-quoted comment about Lukacs and Bloch. See also Michael Löwy, *Georg Lukacs—From Romanticism to Bolshevism* (London, 1979); Idem., *Redemption and Utopia* (Stanford, 1992); and Anson Rabinbach, "Between Enlightenment and Apocalypse: Benjamin, Bloch and Modern German Jewish Messianism," *New German Critique* 34 (1985) 78–125.

33. Markus, 98.

34. On Lukacs's Jewish roots, see Lukacs, *Record of a Life*, 26–27, 29, 144.

35. For an excellent account of the work, see Andrew Arato and Paul Breines, *The Young Lukacs and the Origins of Western Marxism* (New York, 1979), 13–32.

36. See Congdon, 48.

37. For analysis and discussion of the collection, see Congdon 48–52 and 62–65 and especially Markus, 99–110.

38. Lukacs, *Soul and Form* (Cambridge, 1974), 28.

39. See Lukacs, *Selected Correspondence 1902–1920* (New York, 1986), letters 65–66 (February 1, 1911), 143–149.

40. Lukacs, *Soul and Form*, 28.

41. Ibid., 29, 41.

42. Ibid., 31.

43. Ibid., 36.

44. Ibid., 40.

45. See Congdon, 58–59; the essay also appeared in German in *Logos*, Volume 2, in 1911. In the same issue of *A Szellem* Lukacs published a brief, laudatory review of Buber's two books on Hasidism; his interest in mysticism permeates the longer essay as well and is tied to the tragic situation that he seeks to explore, See Congdon, 60.

46. Lukacs, *Soul and form*, 153.

47. Ibid., 158.

48. On the contrast, see Ibid., 149–162.

49. Congdon, 66–69.

50. See Ibid., 43–48.

51. Lukacs, *Selected Correspondence*, 54–57.

52. Lukacs, "On Poverty of Spirit," *The Philosophical Forum* 3, 3–4 (Spring–Summer, 1978) 371–85.

53. Ibid., 373–76, 377.

54. Ibid., 381–84.

55. See Congdon, 67–69; also, Löwy, *Redemption and Utopia*, 102–109.

56. In the years just prior to his death, 1922–23 or so, Kafka may have found some morsel of optimism and hope, but the bulk of his writings exhibit little of it, or as Benjamin puts it, there is hope but not for us.

57. It marked a transformation in Kafka's literary and intellectual career and expressed the powerful struggle within him concerning his relationship with Felice Bauer, his father and family, his art, and his work. By December, he had interrupted feverish activity on a novel—which became *Amerika*—to write again about the tension between his writing, his art, and everyday life; the result was dramatic—the story "Metamorphosis."

58. Stanley Corngold (trans. & ed.) in Franz Kafka, *The Metamorphosis* (New York, 1972), xiv–xvi.

59. On this section, see Robert Alter, *Necessary Angels: Tradition and Modernity in Kafka, Benjamin, and Scholem* (Cambridge, 1991); and especially Marthe Robert's excellent book, *Franz Kafka's Loneliness* (London, 1982). Also see Richie Robertson, *Kafka: Judaism, Politics and Literature* (Oxford, 1985) and the biographies by Ronald Hayman, *Kafka: A Biography* (New

York, 1981) and Ernst Pawel, *The Nightmare of Reason: A Life of Franz Kafka* (New York, 1984).

60. Robert, 27.

61. Kafka, *Letter to His Father* (New York, 1966) 75–83.

62. See Robert, 47–61; Pawel, 238–250; and Hayman. Indeed , he was so taken with Löwy and Yiddish drama that he personally arranged for Löwy a one-man-show in Town Hall on February 18, 1912, for which he prepared and delivered and introduction on the Yiddish language; see Kafka, "An Introductory Talk on the Yiddish Language," in Mark Anderson, ed., *Reading Kafka: Prague, Politics and the Fin de Siècle* (New York, 1989), 263–66.

63. Robert, 53–54.

64. Ibid., 60. On the romanticizing of the Eastern Jew in Europe, see Steven E. Aschheim's excellent book, *Brothers and Strangers: The East European Jew in German and German Jewish consciousness 1800–1923* (Madison, 1982).

65. Pawel, 240.

66. See William C. Rubenstein, "A report to an Academy," in Angel Flores and Homer Swander ed., *Franz Kafka Today* (Madison, 1964), 5–60.

67. Clement Greenberg, "At the Building of the Great Wall of China," in *Franz Kafka Today*, 77–81; Robertson, 172–76.

68. See Bauber's "Two Types of Faith" and Rosenzweig's letter in Nahum N. Glatzer, trans. & ed., *Franz Rosenzweig: His Life and Thought* (New York, 1961); also see Scholem's fragments, discussed by David Biale and the correspondence between Scholem and Benjamin of the 1930s on Kafka, revelation, and mysticism in Gershom Scholem, ed., *The Correspondence of Walter Benjamin and Gershom Scholem 1932–1940* (New York, 1989) and in Scholem and Theodor W. Adorno, eds., *The Correspondence of Walter Benjamin 1910–1940* (Chicago, 1994).

69. Walter Benjamin, *Illuminations*(London, 1977), 147. From a letter to Scholem, June 12, 1938. For excellent comments on this passage, see the review article on Benjamin by David Stern, "The Man With Qualities: The Incongruous Achievement of Walter Benjamin," *The New Republic* (April 10, 1995), 31–8.

70. Ibid., 148.

71. Benjamin spent a great deal of time reflecting on Kafka's work, and to a degree he seems to have identified with him. For significant discussion, see Alter; Susan A Handelman, *Fragments of Redemption: Jewish Thought and Literary Theory in Benjamin, Scholem, and Levinas* (Bloomington, 1991), Corngold and Michael Jennings, "Walter Benjamin/Gershom Scholem," *Interpretation* 12 (1984) 357–66.

72. Among discussions I have found especially helpful are Löwy, *Redemption and Utopia*; Rabinbach; Alter; Corngold and Jennings; Richard Wolin, *Walter Benjamin: An Aesthetic of Redemption* (New York, 1982) and most of all the books by Jennings, *Dialectical Images: Walter Benjamin's Theory of Literary*

Criticism (Ithaca, 1987) and John McCole, *Walter Benjamin and the Antinomies of Tradition* (Ithaca, 1993). The best source on Benjamin's life, outside of the letters and the correspondence with Scholem, is Bernd Witte, *Walter Benjamin: An Intellectual Biography* (Detroit, 1991).

73. Benjamin, *Reflections* (New York, 1978), 18; cf. Witte, 33–34.

74. See Scholem, *Walter Benjamin: The Story of a Friendship* (Philadelphia, 1981), 91; Jennings, 58–59; Corngold and Jennings, 359–60. The piece could very well be a note in preparation for Benjamin's review of Ernst Bloch's *Geist der Utopie*, which was completed in 1920, never published, and lost.

75. Corngold and Jennings, 359.

76. Benjamin, *Reflections*, 312.

77. See Idem., *Illuminations*, 265–66.

78. Jennings, 187.

79. Ibid., 207, 208; see Benjamin, *Illuminations*, 257.

80. Jennings, 209.

81. Ibid., 7.

82. See McCole, 63–67, 106–110.

83. See Jennings, 38, 46–47; The critic must "blast a specific era out of the homogeneous course of history"; see also Benjamin, *Illuminations*, 265; Idem., "N[Re The Theory of Knowledge, Theory of Progress]," in Gary Smith, ed., *Benjamin: Philosophy, Aesthetics, History* (Chicago, 1989), 38–83; and McCole.

84. In the fragments from the Arcades Project, see N 10,3 and N 10a,3 (in *Benjamin: Philosophy, Aesthetics, History*, 66–67).

85. Also, according to Peter Osborne, there is redemption of history as a whole, but this may be a metaphor. See "Small-scale Victories, Large-Scale Defeats: Walter Benjamin's Politics of Time," in Andrew Benjamin and Peter Osborne, eds., *Walter Benjamin's Philosophy* (London, 1994), 59–109.

86. Benjamin, *Illuminations*, 256.

87. See Jennings, 58–62, especially 60.

88. Benjamin, *Illuminations*, 265.

89. Ibid., 263.

90. Ibid., 257–59.

91. Ibid., 263.

92. Ibid., 265.

93. See Osborne, 83.

94. See Rabinbach; and Osborne, 59–60 and n.8.

95. Jürgen Habermas, "Walter Benjamin: Consciousness-Raising or Rescuing Critique," in Gary Smith, ed., *On Walter Benjamin* (Cambridge, 1988), 118. Cf. Jennings, 37–39.

96. Habermas, 160. For Benjamin, it seems that revolutionary action involves something more than an understanding of truth. But it is not clear what Benjamin thinks this something more might be.

97. See Stephan Moses, "Walter Benjamin and Franz Rosenzweig," in *Benjamin: Philosophy, Aesthetics, History*, 228–46.

98. For discussion, see Ibid., 241–44.

99. See "The Builders," in Glatzer, 292.

100. Ibid., 302–3 (from Part Three of "The Star").

101. Franz Rosenzweig, *The Star of Redemption* (New York, 1970), 323.

DIFFICULT LIBERTY: THE BASIS OF COMMUNITY IN EMMANUEL LEVINAS

William V. Rowe

I. Introductory Remarks

In order to mark a kind of destination for my reflections, I begin with a remark taken from Emmanuel Levinas' collection of essays entitled *Difficult Liberty*.

> The salvation of human universality perhaps once more requires paths that do not lead to the great metropolis. Tongues are once again confused. . . . The age of Abraham has returned.[1]

My topic in this essay is the philosophy of community in Emmanuel Levinas. I have two aims. The first is to say something about Levinas' philosophy in general—or I should say his thinking, since only part of this dignified and compelling work should be called a "philosophy." My second aim is to make a sensible connection between this philosophy and the central theme of our volume, *From Ghetto to Emancipation*. I will combine these aims by taking the themes of ghetto and emancipation as one way the entire thought of Levinas may be approached. But in order to do this, the problems of ghetto and emancipation must be formulated in the right way.

II. Definitions

Let us understand "emancipation," with all of its complexity as an historical movement, to signify nothing less than the Western Enlightenment as experienced by Jewish communities in Europe, especially in the nineteenth century.

The term "ghetto" is more difficult to define because it conceals a plurality of senses. In the title of the present volume ghetto refers in the first place to the isolated and premodern life of Jewish communities before the Enlightenment. But there are other senses.

Our volume title also echoes the essay in which Salo Baron rejects the common, negative image of the medieval Jewish ghetto,[2] a rejection that exposes emancipation to a new perspective and brings to light another ghetto present in emancipation itself. I believe Levinas is indispensable to an understanding of this second ghetto. By the same token, a third, post-Enlightenment ghetto culminating in Nazism, is indispensable to an understanding of Levinas.

The second ghetto is that which emancipation itself created in the life of emancipated Jews, a process that ushered modern Jews into a ghetto of a different kind. The third ghetto is the reactionary and anti-Semitic ghetto that is based on the failure of emancipation—a failure that is more than, but includes, the failure of assimilation—a failure Levinas refers to as "the end of philosophy."[3] The third ghetto is associated with the anti-Enlightenment movements of Communism, Fascism, and Nazism.

As important as this third ghetto is for Levinas I would like to focus on the second ghetto, because for Levinas it is the root of the problem. Or, at least, it is here in the second ghetto that we are confronted—I should say, that contemporary Judaism is confronted—with its greatest challenge. That challenge is the justification, the restoration, the redemption, of universality[4] and hence of pluralism, which the West has so far known in the rather bland—that is, melting pot—terms of the Enlightenment with its notion of tolerance. As Adriaan Peperzak says in his 1993 book on the thought of Levinas,

> Is not one of the features by which our civilization is simultaneously great and weak precisely its ability to maintain a more or less peaceful community of radically divergent traditions and histories? The price paid for our moral and ideological pluralism seems to lie in the superficiality or even the emptiness of our general culture as illustrated by the media. Is this price too high for peace?[5]

We might say that the challenge of the so-called second ghetto for Judaism—or for Jews in their Jewishness—is to recover or resurrect from out of Biblical and Talmudic sources a basis for universal human community that does not wash out, or melt together, differences, or above all, that does not eliminate, but rather assumes responsibility for, what Levinas calls the Other.

III. The Ghetto of Private Religion

The universalism and pluralism—in short, the tolerance—of Enlightenment emancipation would not have seemed plausible, indeed would not have been possible, without the invention or discovery of the "private." The private in this context, means more than the intimate sphere of friendship, love, and personal identity. It means the entire domain of non- or prepublic life.

A defining moment in the history of the concept of tolerance, and hence of privacy, is Kant's essay, "What Is Enlightenment?"[6] Kant derives tolerance from respect for the moral law. The moral law is simply reason, but reason may be used in a public or private way. For the sake of enlightenment the public use of reason must enjoy unrestricted freedom, Kant argues. But in its private use, for example in the sphere of religious belief, reason may suffer restrictions of many kinds without threatening reason as such.

In the nineteenth–century nomenclature of John Stuart Mill the private is opposed to the public as the "self-regarding virtues" are opposed to the "other-regarding virtues."[7] It is the restriction of certain things to the private realm that underlies and makes possible the tolerance of emancipation. Following Mill we could define tolerance as one's other-directed regard for the self-regard of another. Tolerance becomes possible as soon as certain things become private, and emancipation becomes possible on the basis of tolerance.

Enlightenment tolerance emancipated Jews from the first ghetto. But the so-called "private" sphere of prepublic life became, for European Jews, a second ghetto because it represented the effective isolation not of Jews, but of their Judaism from Western life and even from the lives of emancipated Jews themselves. Jews entered the second ghetto on the day that Judaism became a "religion," a critical category for Enlightenment emancipation, one which designated a private matter which does not affect the life of the citizen as citizen and which merely involves a person's experience of or contact with something called "the sacred." Such experience, Enlightenment thinkers argued, must be present if society is to survive, but it must not be cultivated by public institutions if these institutions are to remain universal, hence the blandness of this public universality. Meanwhile, the differences between individual encounters with the sacred require mutual tolerance. Levinas remarks,

> From this point on, Jewish education becomes religious instruction in which ideas, detached from the civilization that nurtured them, express, in abstract and bloodless form, the ultimate difference still separating Jews from the homogeneous society into which they had entered . . .[8]

This second ghetto is perhaps rather spiritual or even metaphorical in comparison to the real, social isolation of the medieval pale or ghetto. But it was just as effective in neutralizing the influence of Judaism—without eliminating the impact of Jewishness—on Western society. Christianity found the privatizing category of religion acceptable because at the time of the Enlightenment Western social life was still dominated by Christian forms that were considered permanent because centuries of tradition stood behind them. Furthermore, the Enlightenment category of religion seemed to be calculated, in part, to quell conflicts between Protestant and Catholic Christians or even between different strains of Protestantism. Some of Leibniz's political writings exhibit this strategy.[9] We are tempted to conclude that the modern category of religion is a secularized Christian idea. Certainly the dominant philosophies of religion in the last century have assumed the category of religion in the modern sense, and in most of them Judaism comes off badly as a less than perfect example of the class, while Christianity emerges as its highest realization.[10]

IV. Is Judaism a Religion?

The point we must notice in order to understand Levinas is that Judaism is not a member of the class of things the Enlightenment called religion. Levinas quotes with approval Franz Rosenzweig's remark that "the good Lord did not create religion, he created the world."[11] Judaism is nothing "private"; it is not apolitical; it cannot survive when separated from the vital and public questions of a living community. Above all, for Levinas, Judaism does not concern itself with the "sacred." This is a point Levinas especially emphasizes as he carefully distinguishes between the sacred on the one hand and the holy on the other. The idea of the sacred is forever linked to the numinous (to use Rudolf Otto's term) and relates to the overwhelming and intimidating power of Being or of the totality that confronts and limits the worshipper. The idea of the holy, on the other hand, is ethical and concerns one's responsibility to and for the Other.

But there is a more satisfactory way to express this point concerning religion, and that would be to replace the private or confessional definition with another more holistic one. One would then define religion as life itself, or as the relation—Levinas will call it the "pulsation"—of life toward God. In this sense it is life, and not some compartment of life, that is "religion." This is in fact how Levinas has learned from Rosenzweig to speak:

> Religion, before being a confession, is the very pulsation of life in which God enters into a relationship with Man, and Man with the World. Religion, like the web of life, is anterior to the philosopher's totality.[12]

But this new sense of religion is not only holistic, it is earthly.

> Is Judaism not different from the religions it has spawned [Christianity and Islam] in that it questions whether personal salvation can be something distinct from the redemption of the visible world? . . . Judaism unites men in an ideal of terrestrial justice in which the Messiah represents a promise and a fulfillment. Ethics is its primordial religious emotion. It does not found a church for trans-ethical ends.[13]

Now it is in this sense that Levinas says Judaism is a religion. But it is a sense of religion that can only emerge at the end of philosophy—in the sense mentioned above—that is, after the failures of assimilation, Enlightenment, emancipation, and of the universality based upon tolerance toward the private. Levinas sometimes refers to Enlightenment universality, which is rooted in a philosophically or conceptually perceived commonness, as *totalité*. To this he contrasts an utterly different form of universality and community, which he calls *l'infini*, the Infinite, or simply Infinity.

V. Religion as Sociality or Being-for-the-Other

By means of this ethical notion of the holy, or of Infinity, Levinas has attempted to restore the idea of sociality to a central position in philosophy, and he bases this attempt on the centrality of sociality in Judaism. It is sociality that renders Judaism earthly; it is sociality that makes the justice sought by Judaism something "terrestrial."

One follows the Most High God, above all by drawing near to one's fellow man, and showing concern for "the widow, the orphan, the stranger and the beggar," an approach that must not be made "with empty hands." It is therefore on earth, amongst men, that the spirit's adventure unfolds.[14]

By sociality and terrestrial justice, however, Levinas does not mean that philosophy, and above all ethics and every thought directed toward the good, is somehow made relative to society. Sociality does not represent a human collective gathered through time and confined to a "place," from which it arose as from native soil and on which it enjoys the autochthony of *Lebensraum*. Nor does sociality signify the intimacy of the one-to-one relation of friendship, which might strike us as the only other alternative when we speak of sociality, and which appears to be the form of human relation that Buber made central to his thought.

Sociality in Levinas' thinking is the experience of the face of the Other; it is difficult liberty. Levinas is not concerned with the possibility or impossibility of liberty, but with its capacity to take upon itself a burden of responsibility for the Other. The polarity that runs throughout Levinas' thinking is not a polarity that opposes freedom to unfreedom but one that opposes responsible to irresponsible freedom, difficult freedom to a freedom without obligations, responsibility to simple self-assertion. The experience of the Other or the face of the Other gives freedom a responsibility that reaches beyond the imperative of maintaining its own power, a responsibility that justifies freedom, and indeed transforms and elevates freedom into justice. Without this vocation freedom drifts into a vortex of self-determination and, therefore, will-to-power.

VI. Freedom and the Other

As Levinas explains it, it is not a question of limiting freedom through confrontation with the Other. That, of course, is the pattern of classical liberalism: a state of war exists prior to the founding of society, a state of war we escape through a contract with others. Through this contract we limit our freedom by joining our purposes—which is to say our freedom—with that of others in civil society.

Levinas' Other, however, does not confront the self with another self—an alter ego. It does not confront my freedom with an external freedom nor does it oppose my power to another power. Rather, by Other, Levinas means a confrontation with something beyond freedom and beyond power. That "beyond" is displayed in powerlessness. When I perceive, in my interactions with others, their weakness and powerlessness, and therefore perceive the possibilities of abuse of power on my part, then my freedom becomes difficult. That experience of the face of the Other is the source of everything ethical; it is the basis of community; it is original sociality. Says Levinas,

> No rights can ensue from the simple fact that a person needs *espace vital* [*Lebensraum*]. The consciousness of my I reveals no right to me. My freedom shows itself to be arbitrary. It appeals to an investiture. The "normal" exercise of my ego, which transforms into "mine" everything it can reach and touch, is put in question . . . To be oneself [*pour soi*] is already to know the fault I have committed with regard to the Other. But the fact that I do not quiz myself on the Other's rights paradoxically indicates that the Other is not a new edition of myself; in its Otherness it is situated in a dimension of height, in the idea, the Divine, and through my relation to the Other, I am in touch with God.[15]

The origin of every obligation is the experience of the face of the Other. It is the Other in the vulnerability, the nudity of his face that renders me *obligé*—obliged—subject to obligation. Obligation in this sense is done unto me by the Other and I suffer its imposition. This suffering, this passion, this passivity, is responsibility. It is this experience that constitutes the difficulty of my freedom, an experience of sociality more primordial and more fundamentally ethical than that of friendship (the meeting of I and Thou) or of social cooperation.

But it will never be enough to camp at the foot of the Mount of Obligation in the shadow of the face. We must also hear the commandment, for to experience the face or vulnerability of the Other is to hear the word, "Thou shalt not kill." For Levinas, this word is not one of the commandments; it is the whole law. It expresses Hillel's summary of the Torah: Do not do to the other what you would not have the other do to you. The face of the Other, which is elevated in a dimension of height, is the Sinai known by everyone acquainted with wandering in the wilderness. But of course to hear the Torah is not enough; one must also talk the Torah through, that is, bring its speech into my speech, our speech. If I may use this analogy, the "Torah" heard in the presence of the Other and seen in his face must be supplemented by the "Talmud" of a practical and social philosophizing whose principles—I mean, whose beginnings—are no longer the Greek ones of *phronesis, philia,* and *polis*: Insight, Friendship, and City, taking city to mean the human community as self-related totality. But what other kind of community is there?

VII. Two Forms of Community

For Levinas there are two socialities, two forms of community, rooted in two religiosities. There is the sociality of the first person plural, the community of the We or the Us, and then there is the sociality of the third person singular, the community of the He or the Other.

All of the questions surrounding the first kind of community are questions of inclusion and belonging. That is because the We contains both I and Thou. Inclusion and belonging involve the sharing of a commonness. Sharing is a being with another, a *Mitsein* or *Mitdasein* as Heidegger would say.[16] What drives or motivates sharing for Levinas is need, that is, self-insufficiency. Correlative to need or insufficiency in the individual is the conception of community as self-sufficiency, a characterization that appears to fit the social philosophy of Aristotle.[17] The community of the We is therefore something like an expansion of the I. We, although plural, is still the first person. We as community is still a form of self-concern, a form of *Sorge* or Care for our Being, as Heidegger again would say. The telos of the community of the We is that of being truly ourselves or, one might say, its aim is identity, authenticity.

The experience of the Other, however, is not a "being with" but a "being for" the Other. It therefore founds a community whose roots are beyond Being. The Other, whose name is given in the third person in order to set him off from the We, is the stranger, the widow, the orphan, the one who does not belong to Us. For that reason the kind of sociality invoked in the experience of the Other transcends the sociality of the We, with its traditions, its virtues, its stories. This genuine sociality is a transcendence; it is metaphysical. If sociality is something ethical, nevertheless the community of the Other does not have the kind of ethics that rests merely upon the making and the telling of stories. It does not have the kind of goodness that knows itself simply through the immanent categories of virtue, which always refer goodness back to the *vir* of man and the *vis* of his power.

True sociality—that is to say, justice—is not to be confused with that of mythomorphic societies which owe their power to include, their force of inclusivity, their will-to-assimilation, to their members' habit of yielding to a story that is a mythos of the sacred totality. In fundamental opposition to the religiosity of the sacred totality and in stark contrast to every totalitarian We, Levinas asserts the infinity of responsibility for the Other. If this responsibility is given the form of speech or discourse—or of Saying, as Levinas prefers to put it—then this discourse is not the telling of a story, but the experience of an interruption of one's story by the voice of the Other. Such interruption—the eruption into my ears of the voice of the Other—is speech, discourse, the Saying of the Other. For myth or story rounds out and totalizes. It domesticates otherness by comprehending it within its economy. Like "history" story is a totality in which everything finds its place and nothing is placeless, or out of place, the way the Other as widow, orphan, beggar, always is. When story tells of the stranger the stranger ceases to be strange; story is the end of the Other. This of course is not said of every possible story, but of story that is myth, that is, story that charms and enthralls, story that avoids the address of the Other.

What Levinas calls discourse or speech, however, is not the end of the Other. Rather, the Other is the end—in a different sense of end—of speech. Speech is *for* the Other.[18] The experience of the Other, therefore, interrupts virtues and stories, traditions and every native language. For when the Other speaks, he speaks otherwise than We. The Other's speech is the interruption of Our life by means of a transcendent, and therefore absolute, claim. It is this interruption which makes life a pulsution. Levinas' Other is the human being I encounter as stranger sent to me, as it were, by God—the Other behind the Other, the other Other—so that the confrontation with him, like the confrontation of the Good Samaritan with the injured Israelite in the New Testament parable, is immediately a relation with God. I and Other share no membership in a common totality that embraces us both. Consequently, my relation to the Other is not symmetrical so that through my power I could impose on the Other the obligation which the Other through his weakness imposes on me. The Other comes from elsewhere.

VIII. A New Universality

But despite this opposition between the two forms of community, Levinas would see the Sinai of the Other as the beginning of a new kind of We, a new universality, a new idea of the community of man. In the Other is a true universality. Just as the confrontation with the Other does not eliminate or even limit freedom but challenges it and causes it to become obliged, so the Infinity of the Other does not subvert every totality.

Levinas' first great work in philosophy is his 1961 *Totality and Infinity*.[19] We do well to notice the "and" in this title. For Levinas does not say "Totality versus Infinity" or "Totality and Infinity in Dialectical Tension." What Levinas is "against" is not totality, but totalitarianism, which is totality unaccompanied and unjustified by recognition of the Other, an unredeemed universality. The whole point would be to bring infinity and totality together, to have an Us, to have virtues, to have traditions, to tell stories, but justified virtues, and justified stories. It would be tempting, even natural, to infer that a justified tradition, or justified story, is one that includes otherness of the Other. But an included Other is Other no more. What Levinas implies is that justified traditions are those that do not exist for Us but for the Other.

Hence traditions that give the final word to tradition, to belonging, to unity and community, traditions that give the final word to virtue, are deficient in sociality because the desire for, and responsibility to, the Other is absent in them. In such traditions the community is considered autochthonous (in other words, rooted in a native soil) and autonomous in its simplicity and self-relation. For that reason such traditions become mythic, which means that they speak of themselves through story, but cannot be spoken to by the Other. The journey of such communities is an Odyssey, which is always a journey home, a journey toward one's native soil. How different is the journey—or rather sojourn—of Abraham, a journey away from what is one's own, a journey begun by a call out of one's native territory, a journey toward another land that is not my own!

In *Survival in Auschwitz*,[20] Primo Levi describes how the Nazi death camps imposed the ethos of the perpetrators upon the victims. In the search for survival in the camps prisoners quickly moved into a space beyond good and evil. Among the prisoners of the camps, he writes, there were not good and evil persons; there were the drowned and the saved. To become one of the saved one had to become committed to oneself and exclude concern for the Other. But there are hints in his essays of other possibilities and other interpretations. It is Edith Wyschogrod, a student of Levinas' writings, who in an essay entitled "Concentration Camps and the End of the Life World"[21] picks up on these other possibilities and builds on Levinas' notion of responsibility for the Other.

Wyschogrod describes that point at which responsibility for the Other emerged in the camp and transformed it—for some individuals—into an ethical world. That was the moment when survival became the more difficult of two things, being saved and being drowned. That, she argues, was always the point at which survival became meaningful for someone other than the survivor, the point at which survival mattered because of the necessity to testify, to bear witness, to ensure that the world should know and not forget. In such a situation, to survive—to seek to survive—was not a commitment to oneself or an exclusion of the Other. On the contrary, it meant a vigilant and daily sacrifice. It was sacrificial survival, a survival for the Other.

With this point in mind I close with a passage from an article in *Difficult Freedom* entitled simply, "Judaism."

> The traumatic experience of my slavery in Egypt constitutes my very humanity, a fact that immediately allies me to the workers, the wretched, and the persecuted peoples of the world. My uniqueness lies in the responsibility I display for the other. I cannot fail in my duty towards any man, any more than I can have someone else stand in for my death . . . Man is therefore indispensable to God's plans within being. This leads to the idea of being chosen, which can degenerate into that of pride but which originally expresses the awareness of an indisputable assignation from which an ethics springs and through which the universality of the end being pursued involves the solitude and isolation of the individual responsible. [22]

NOTES

1.   Emmanuel Levinas, "Antihumanism and Education," *Difficult Freedom*, translated by Sean Hand (Baltimore, 1990), 288.

2.   Salo Baron, "Ghetto and Emancipation: Shall We Revise the Traditional View?," *The Menorah Journal* 14 (June 1928), 515–526.

3.   Emmanuel Levinas, "Between Two Worlds," *Difficult Freedom*, 185f. "The end of philosophy . . . the movement that led to the liberation of man enslaves man within the system which he builds. In the State and nationalisms, in the socialist statism that emerges from philosophy, the individual experiences the necessity of philosophical totality as a totalitarian tyranny" (186).

4. Levinas referred to this, in our first quotation above, as "the salvation of human universality." See note number 1.

5. Adriaan Peperzak, *An Introduction to the Philosophy of Emmanuel Levinas* (West Lafayette, Indiana, 1993), 9.

6. See Immanuel Kant, *Philosophical Writings*, translated by Ernst Behler (New York, 1986).

7. John Stuart Mill, *On Liberty* (New York, 1947), 76ff.

8. Levinas, "Antihumanism and Education," 280.

9. See E. J. Aiton, *Leibniz: A Biography* (Briston, 1985), 123–125, regarding Leibniz's distinction between interior and exterior communion among believers. See also Leroy E. Loemker, *Struggle for Synthesis: the Seventeenth Century Background of Leibniz's Synthesis of Order and Freedom* (Cambridge, Mass., 1972), 82–5.

10. See Rudolf Otto, *The Idea of the Holy*, translated by John W. Harvey (Oxford, 1969), and Gerardus van der Leeuw, *Religion in Essence and Manifestation*, translated by J. E. Turner (New York, 1963).

11. Levinas, "Between Two Worlds," 186.

12. Ibid., 189.

13. Levinas, "Judaism and the Present," *Difficult Freedom*, 210–11.

14. Levinas, "Judaism," *Difficult Freedom*, 26.

15. Levinas, "A Religion for Adults," *Difficult Freedom*, 17.

16. Martin Heidegger, *Being and Time*, translated by John MacQuarrie and Edward Robinson (New York, 1962), 153–63.

17. Aristotle, *Nicomachean Ethics*, translated by Martin Ostwald (New York, 1962), Book I, Chapters 2 and 7.

18. But strictly speaking, for Levinas, I may not say the Other is a telos. For a telos brings a being to its completion, the actualization of its potential, the fulfillment of its *conatus essendi* , its perfection as totality. Telos belongs to being. The Other, however, is beyond being and, therefore, precisely not a telos.

19. Levinas, *Totality and Infinity: An Essay on Exteriority*, translated by Alphonso Lingis (Pittsburgh, 1969).

20. Primo Levi, *Survival in Auschwitz*, translated by Stuart Woolf (New York, 1986); see the chapter, "The Drowned and the Saved."

21. Edith Wyschogrod, "Concentration Camps and the End of the Life World," *Echoes From the Holocaust: Philosophical Reflections on a Dark Time*, edited by Alan Rosenberg and Gerald E. Myers (Philadelphia, 1988), 327–40.

22. Livinas, "Judaism," 26.

THE PUZZLING PERSISTENCE OF COMMUNITY: THE CASES OF AIRMONT AND KIRYAS JOEL[1]

Nomi Maya Stolzenberg

T he suburbs of America have changed. Long a site of cultural homogenization, they have become host to an increasingly diverse array of racial and ethnic groups. Immigrants from such countries as Haiti, Jamaica, Guatemala, and El Salvador have formed their own cultural outposts in areas that were formerly enclaves for predominantly white, middle-class aspirants of the American dream.[2] But rather than assimilate into the bland, undifferentiated cultural landscape stereotypically associated with suburban life, many of these groups have proven to be remarkably tenacious in maintaining traditional customs, languages, and lifestyles that distinguish them from other groups.[3] In this dynamic environment, no group has stood out more or displayed more of an inclination for cultural and political autonomy than the various Hasidic Jewish communities which have been moving out of New York City into the neighboring suburban counties for several decades. A new local radio station in Rockland County is emblematic of the demographic shifts: WLIR-AM advertises itself as "all Jewish all the time," but from Friday night through Saturday, in observance of the Jewish Sabbath, it plays Latin and Haitian music.

The resurgence of particularistic groups as exclusive and traditionalist as the Hasidim is puzzling, if one accepts the notion that modern, liberal principles of political organization inexorably lead to assimilation and the demise of traditional, close-knit communities. The basic constitutional principles of liberalism, which posit a split between the political and private realms, have long been viewed as a chief cause of the atomization of holistic communities. It is from this standpoint that the persistence of traditional, separatist forms of community, like that of the Hasidim, appears enigmatic. In a milieu where the practices of local government, including zoning and public education, have historically served to foster secularization and cultural assimilation, the Hasidim living in the suburbs of New York have been strikingly effective in turning the mechanisms of local government to their advantage, even as they have been forced to struggle with considerable local opposition.

A close examination of these contests over local government, including the legal disputes that ensue, presents a picture of the relationship between liberalism and community that differs from the commonplace vision of liberalism's "atomizing" effect. Not that this commonplace is false, but it expresses an oversimplification—a truth, but not the whole truth. Careful analysis of the disputes over local government between the suburban Hasidim and their neighbors reveals that, in addition to posing a threat to traditional communities, liberal principles of government can also serve to protect and empower them.

The possibility that liberal principles might operate to the advantage of an exclusive, separatist, holistic community is illustrated in the recent Supreme Court case of *Kiryas Joel*.[4] *Kiryas Joel* involved a challenge to the constitutionality of a public school district that was created to serve an exclusively Hasidic community. The Supreme Court upheld the challenge, holding that the formation of the Hasidic school district constituted an unconstitutional state establishment of religion. An analysis of *Kiryas Joel* that gives due attention not only to its immediate outcome, but also to the structure of its underlying reasoning, demonstrates that the effects of liberal law upon community are complex. These effects become visible when we juxtapose the case against another legal contest over local government between Orthodox Jews and their neighbors—the case of *United States v. Village of Airmont*.[5] Although *Airmont* raises questions about a newly incorporated village, rather than about the formation of a school district, it is in many respects the mirror image of *Kiryas Joel* as it involves a political secession from a larger town by a group of residents who sought to minimize the presence and political influence of Orthodox and Hasidic Jews. Like *Kiryas Joel*, it rests on legal reasoning that implicitly justifies the incorporation of an exclusionary local government under certain circumstances.

The *Airmont* litigation serves as a particularly useful point of comparison because it arose out of the same general milieu as *Kiryas Joel*. *Airmont* is one of a host of civil and criminal cases that deal with the growing tensions between traditionally observant Jews and their secular neighbors in the suburbs of New York.[6] Airmont lies in Rockland County, New York, which is adjacent to Orange County, the home of Kiryas Joel. In their exodus out of New York City, various Hasidic groups established separate footholds in different towns in Orange and Rockland Counties. Simultaneously, non-Hasidic Orthodox Jews also flocked to the suburbs, where, within close proximity to New York, they could escape the travails of city life. Although members zealously guard the boundary-lines dividing the different Hasidic and Orthodox groups, they have found themselves unceremoniously lumped together by their non-Orthodox suburban neighbors when it comes to the question of their compliance with prevailing norms of land use and education.

Two land-use controversies in particular have fueled the antagonism between Orthodox Jews and their opponents. First, many Orthodox and Hasidic Jews object to the single-family zoning requirements typical of the relatively affluent suburbs. Orthodox real estate developers spear-headed the demand to change the zoning laws in order to permit multiple family housing. In some cases, they purchased land and began to advertise "Torah Community" subdivisions containing apartment buildings even before variances from the customary single-family zoning requirements were obtained. In addition to the disagreement over multi-family dwellings, controversies arose over the placement of houses of worship. Some residents raised objections to plans to build new free-standing synagogues. A more pervasive conflict grew out of the newcomers' use of *shtiblekh*, informal worship congregations located in residential homes, which do not comport with customary zoning restrictions on the number, location, and size of houses of worship.

The cases of *Kiryas Joel* and *Airmont* illustrate an ever more popular response to these seemingly intractable disputes: political secession. Towns that embraced increasingly heterogeneous and fractious populations have split apart, as new and smaller local governments were formed by subcommunities seeking a municipality of their own. In the town of Ramapo, which originally contained what is now the village of Airmont, no fewer than twelve communities seceded to form their own separate villages. Both Kiryas Joel and Airmont were created as part of the general movement for secession and village incorporation which swept across Rockland and Orange Counties, New York, and beyond.

The contrast between the two cases raises a question avoided in the *Kiryas Joel* litigation. We will see that a highly formalistic conception of religious neutrality enables exclusively Hasidic local govern-ment—villages *and* public school districts—to be formed and, furthermore, to be constitutionally justified. But that same view of neutrality serves equally well to justify the formation of local governments, like the village of Airmont, which are hostile to traditionalist Jews. Given that the same formalistic jurisprudence underwrites both these results, should the partisans of Jewish communal autonomy support or reject it? And, on the other side, what are the principles of the nonformalistic conception of neutrality that would support the conclusion that religiously exclusive local governments, like Airmont and Kiryas Joel, are constitutionally and legally defective? Confronting these questions opens our eyes to the complexity of liberal legalism's impact on exclusionary communities.

Kiryas Joel and Airmont provide an instructive contrast. Kiryas Joel was formed so that the members of the ultra-Orthodox Satmar sect of Hasidic Judaism could have their own local government, free not only from the competing political demands of non-Jews, but from other Orthodox and Hasidic Jews with whom they differ. Airmont was formed precisely in order to get away from "the Jews" (though some of those who sought this escape were non-Orthodox Jews). The Satmar Hasidim, who created the village of Kiryas Joel, compose the very picture of the tight-knit, pervasively regulated, traditional holistic community that references to *Gemeinschaft* conjure up. In contrast, the founders and inhabitants of Airmont are a loose and shifting assortment of individuals. Kiryas Joel is a religious community; Airmont is secular. Kiryas Joel is homogeneous—100% of its inhabitants are members of the Satmar sect;

Airmont is religiously and ethnically heterogeneous (though predominantly white, professional, and middle to upper-middle class). The community of Kiryas Joel is extremely cohesive, organized around the central figure of the *Rebbe*, the hereditary rabbinic leader who exercises charismatic authority over every aspect of his followers' lives. The residents of Airmont have no unifying organization other than their sporadic and optional involvement in the democratic procedures that state law prescribes for forming and governing local municipalities. Unlike Airmont, Kiryas Joel is fiercely opposed to assimilation and modern innovations.   As the Supreme Court observed, the Satmars "interpret the Torah strictly; segregate the sexes outside the home; speak Yiddish as their primary language; eschew television, radio, and English-language publications; and dress in distinctive ways that include head coverings and special garments for boys and modest dresses for girls."[7] Adult men wear long beards, sidelocks, and the dark frockcoats and hats of late nineteenth–century Hungary.[8] Adult women dress modestly and cover their heads with scarves and wigs. In short, they look and act differently from most Americans, whereas Airmont residents conform to mainstream cultural norms.

Yet the communities are similar in one important respect. Both are exclusionary. The Satmars resist the penetration of the outside culture; Airmont's inhabitants resist the inclusion of the traditional Jewish way of life. Moreover—and this is the key point for purposes of under-standing liberalism's impact upon community—both communities use the coercive powers of collective regulation to secure and conserve their respectively favored ways of life. Not only is each community able to exercise considerable power over how land will be used (and hence by whom) through the coordinated exercise of individual rights of private property and contract, but each community has also been able to use the powers of local government toward its exclusionary ends. The questions that remain to be explored are how such exclusionary groups are able to assume the form, and command the levers of an official governmental body—i.e., a municipal incorporation or a public school district—and how such results have been justified as being consistent with the requirements of a liberal constitutional order.

Answers to these questions are suggested by the judicial opinions issued in *Airmont* and *Kiryas Joel*. These opinions exhibit four specific modes of liberal legal reasoning that are commonly employed in interpreting the requirements of anti-discrimination and anti-establishment law. Each of these modes of reasoning takes the form of a conceptual distinction: the distinction between (1) public and private realms, which has historically played a central role in liberal thought; (2) religious and nonreligious "cultural" or "secular" domains; (3) neutral *intentions* and neutral *effects*, a distinction more technical and perhaps less familiar, to the reader who is not versed in legal doctrine or political theory; and (4), probably the least familiar of all, laws or mechanisms of government that are *generally* available to all groups on an equal basis, and laws or governmental mechanisms that are *particularistic*, i.e., that advantage or disadvantage a particular group or groups. The distinction here is not that between the general and the particularistic, but rather between *two different ways of understanding the difference* between general and particularistic governmental action. One we shall call *formalistic*, the other we dub *nonformalistic* for reasons that will become clear in the following pages.

Together, these four conceptual distinctions—public versus private; religious versus secular; neutrality of intent versus neutrality of effect; the formalistic distinction between general and particularistic laws versus a non-formalistic version of the same—explain how, in a liberal constitutional order, the material foundations of exclusionary communities are assembled. Beyond that, they explain how some communities are able to assure their continued survival by capturing their own piece of governmental power, in the form of local government institutions. From this perspective, Airmont and Kiryas Joel appear less as aberrations in the American landscape than as particularly vivid—and, in their legal exposition, particularly explicit—examples of what, after all, is a fairly unexceptional phenomenon of American local democracy: the existence of culturally or religiously homogeneous (and, in that respect, exclusionary) municipal governments and public schools.

The distinction between private individual rights and public governmental power plays a particularly crucial role in explaining the establishment and legitimization of homogeneous, exclusionary communities. It is not simply that groups are permitted to exist in the private realm of market transactions and free association.   The theoretically prior private existence of associations is indispensable to the legal justification of *local governments* that "just happen" to contain and represent religiously or culturally homogeneous populations. The idea that public boundaries sometimes "just happen" to be congruent with the boundaries of "private" communities, and that public and private entities are *not*, therefore, equivalent, was crucial to the reasoning of *Kiryas Joel*. It also played a pivotal, albeit implicit, role in the trial judge's determination in *Airmont* that the *government* of Airmont was not biased against Orthodox and Hasidic Jews, even though many of the "private" citizens who founded it—and were subsequently elected to run it—quite clearly were.

In *Airmont*, the court was called upon to consider whether illegal discrimination against Orthodox and Hasidic Jews was involved in the actions of a newly incorporated village. The federal government joined the litigation in support of the private plaintiffs' complaint that the village of Airmont, and its officers and founders, discriminated against Orthodox Jews, in violation of the Federal Fair Housing Act and the First Amendment. In the end, the trial judge, Gerhard Goettel, exonerated the village of charges of anti-Semitism.   (The decision was eventually overturned by the Court of Appeal.)

Evidence that leaders and supporters of the movement to incorporate Airmont were animated by a desire to separate themselves from the new Orthodox arrivals was abundant. Judge Amalya Kearse, writing for the U.S. Court of Appeals in *Airmont II*, quoted a string of statements made by members of the Airmont Civic Association (ACA), the citizens' organization formed to promote the establishment of Airmont as a separate village. In her summary of findings, she found that:

> Throughout the period prior to Airmont's incorporation, ACA emphasized the need for control over zoning in connection with the desire to keep Orthodox and Hasidic Jews out of the Airmont community.   For example, ACA leaders polled Airmont residents as to their views, and one response, read aloud by ACA leaders at an August 1986 ACA meeting, stated as follows:

[W]hat would be better, for us to loose [*sic*] our homes for a religious sect or for us to live as we have lived for the past 25 years. . . .

. . . [L]et the people in the unincorporated Area of Ramapo, go ahead and fight for what they believe in. Instead of giving up for what we've worked very hard for, to a bunch of people who insist on living in the past. I am not prejudice [*sic*] in any way, shape or form but I [*sic*] *will not* have a hasidic community in my backyard. (Emphasis in the original.)

The minutes of the same meeting forecast "a grim picture of a Hasidic belt from Rockland through Orange & Sullivan counties." At a September 1986 meeting shortly after a Hasidic developer had bought land in the Airmont area, one of those attending referred to that purchase and stated that

> everybody knows . . . why the Airmont Civic Association was formed. What does the Airmont Civic Association and the proposed village plan to do to keep these Hasidum [*sic*] out? (Trial Transcript ("Tr.") at 2989).

The developer testified that in 1987, ACA's original president, James Filenbaum, stated that "the reason of forming this village is to keep people like you out of this neighborhood." (Tr. at 890.) At an ACA meeting in the spring of 1989, shortly after the Airmont area residents had voted for incorporation, the suggestion of one resident that ACA get involved in planting trees was met with

> a lot of grunts and groans from the audience and everything, and I heard Mr. Fletcher [one of ACA's more strident leaders] sitting in the back of the room respond to that by saying, you know, let's face it, the only reason we formed this village is to keep those Jews

from Williamsburg [a Hasidic community in Brooklyn,
New York] out of here. (Tr. at 4031.)[9]

In Judge Kearse's presentation, these words, quoted at length from the
trial transcript, speak for themselves. The trial judge, Gerhard Goettel,
made no mention of them, however. The reason Judge Goettel did not
see fit to introduce this evidence, given such prominence in the appellate
court's opinion, can be gleaned from what he did write in his opinion.

With respect to the plaintiffs' contention "[t]hat the Village of
Airmont has developed a reputation as a community hostile to Orthodox
and Hasidic Jews," Judge Goettel responded, "[i]f it has, it is largely the
result of the lawsuits brought against it by the various plaintiffs and the
extensive publicity plaintiffs have intentionally generated."[10] Judge
Goettel's judgment against the plaintiffs is particularly notable because
it required setting aside part of the jury's verdict, an imposition of
judicial authority which is rarely exercised and subject to severe
constraints. While refusing to render verdicts against the *individual*
defendants who served as the village's elected officials and trustees, the
jury found that the *village* had violated the plaintiffs' constitutional right
to the free exercise of religion, as well as the Fair Housing Act's
prohibition against religious discrimination. Judge Goettel justified
modifying the jury's verdict on the grounds that it was internally
inconsistent. He resolved this "inconsistency" between the jury's
treatment of the village as a corporate political entity and of the
individuals who served as its officials in favor of a blanket verdict of
innocence. In his view, whatever "anti-Orthodox underlay"[11] might be
found could only be ascribed to individuals as such, in their private
capacity, and not to public actions.

An exceedingly formalistic distinction between the public
(government) and the private (individuals) is operative in this reasoning.
Rather than recognize that the individual citizens who mouthed patently
anti-Semitic views were the same individuals who *led* the political
movement for the village's incorporation and then served as its officials,
and rather than draw the inference that the village's new zoning code
would likely be interpreted consistently with these officers' professed
intentions, Judge Goettel dismissed the plaintiffs' complaint on the

ground that it amounts to nothing more than an argument that "the Village was conceived in sin and cannot escape the taint of its illegitimate birth."[12] In other words, whatever preceded the political "birth" of the village is a purely private matter. The use of this metaphor implies that the public and private roles of individual citizens are sharply divided. As a result, statements of bias made by village officials are not attributable to them in their official role, let alone to the government which they represent, in the absence of independent evidence of public discriminatory action. Only on the basis of such a strict public-private bifurcation could Judge Goettel deny that the village's zoning code was adopted, at least in part, in order to thwart the Orthodox and Hasidic community. His implicit reliance on the public-private distinction led him to the equally tacit conclusion that the anti-Semitic remarks of the defendants were, if not technically irrelevant, unworthy of judicial remark.

Airmont I thus illustrates how a strict conceptual compartmentalization of public and private actions works to exculpate a government entity of charges that its motives are discriminatory. In effect, the public-private distinction strips the "taint" of bias from the municipality and its officers by locating it in the emanations of the private realm (in which the same individuals who serve as municipal officers reappear in their private roles). Such a formalistic way of assigning motivations to one side or another of a purely conceptual division of domains denies the realities of local politics, in which voters, vote and officials run for election precisely on the basis of the candidates known "personal" views. It flies in the face of the very idea of active citizenship in a democracy, the object of which is to engage individual citizens in political action, and thereby to blend private and public roles. Recalling the evocative analogy employed by Judge Goettel, it is as if the "birth" of a political jurisdiction did not occur through human processes of intercourse, gestation, midwifery, and delivery, but instead sprang from the *deus ex machina* of a stork's visitation—as if there were no connection between the people and activities bringing about the birth and the subsequent actions of a political entity.

The public-private distinction wórked similarly in the litigation of *Kiryas Joel*. In 1989 Mario Cuomo, then governor of New York, authorized the creation of a new public school district within the confines of an existing suburban village, made up exclusively of members of the ultra-orthodox Satmar sect of Hasidic Judaism.[13] The distinctive character of the village is reflected in the very name that its inhabitants bestowed upon it, when, in 1977, they seceded from the larger, more diverse town of Monroe.[14] They named the newly separated municipal incorporation Kiryas Joel—in Hebrew, "the town of Joel"—after the community's religious leader, *Rebbe* Joel Teitelbaum.[15]

Though the Satmars generally rely upon private religious schools to educate their children, they petitioned the state to authorize the creation of a public school system within the village in order to obtain state-funded special needs education for the community's disabled children. Given the existing constitutional prohibition on providing state funds for private sectarian schools,[16] the existing alternatives were to forfeit the financial subsidy from the state and educate the disabled children in religious schools, or to send them to mainstream regional public schools. With the former option ruled out as being prohibitively expensive, Satmar parents first tried and then rejected the second option on the grounds that exposing their disabled children to a foreign cultural environment was psychologically traumatic, religiously offensive, and disruptive of the children's ability to learn. Of particular concern was the fact that the established public schools do not use Yiddish, the children's mother tongue. It was in response to the community's plea for linguistic, cultural, and religious accommodation that the state granted its petition to form a new public school district, with boundaries perfectly coterminous with the Satmars' village.

The Supreme Court's judgment in *Kiryas Joel* that this state act violated the constitutional prohibition against state "establishments" of religion was widely covered by the media.[17] Many observers insisted that such a ruling was required by the First Amendment's establishment prohibition. To these observers, a contrary ruling would have represented an astounding and lamentable departure from the sacred principle of the separation of religious and public realms. But unbeknownst to most casual observers, the Supreme Court's grounds for striking down the creation of the school district in Kiryas Joel were actually quite narrow, and left open the possibility that new state legislation could be passed, supplying constitutionally valid authorization for a public school district with precisely the same geographic boundaries and constituency. The interpretation of the establishment clause articulated in *Kiryas Joel*, which underwrites this possible result, reflects a highly formalistic conception of state neutrality which, in fact, allows religiously exclusive groups to incorporate themselves as local governments, while it simultaneously affirms the sacred principle of the separation of religious and public realms.[18]

As in *Airmont I*, the public-private distinction functions in the reasoning of *Kiryas Joel* to shift the blame for acts of religious exclusion away from public actors by locating them in the "private" realm. This use of the public-private distinction appears most clearly in the Court's acceptance of the constitutionality of the *village* of Kiryas Joel and in its suggestions for how a constitutionally valid school district in Kiryas Joel might be created. In brief, the Supreme Court's reasoning appears to be this: Boundaries of political jurisdictions that are drawn along religious lines violate the establishment clause of the Constitution. Political boundaries that are drawn along other lines, e.g., territorial or geographic, do not violate the establishment clause. But what does it mean to draw a boundary "along" religious lines? If a state act explicitly invokes a religious criterion, i.e., membership in a particular religion or adherence to certain religious practices or beliefs, as the basis for political line-drawing, that is clearly a violation of the establishment clause. But in most cases, the state does not expressly rely on such religious criteria on the face of its authorizing statutes. If a state act does not make religious criteria an *express* basis for political line-drawing, but, for example, articulates a strictly territorial basis which nonetheless *coincides* with the boundaries of a religiously exclusive community, does that violate the establishment clause? This was the problem confronted by the Supreme Court in *Kiryas Joel*. In this case, it found that the state had delegated its "discretionary authority over public schools to a group defined by its character as a religious community,"[19] even though the state did not delegate this power "by express reference to the religious belief of the Satmar community, but to residents of the 'territory of the village of Kiryas Joel.'"[20] The Court concluded that the Act authorizing the public school was "substantially equivalent to defining a political subdivision . . . by a religious test" because it was *intentionally* drawn to exclude all but Satmars.[21] This raises the question of why the village of Kiryas Joel was not found to be similarly constitutionally defective, since it, too, was deliberately formed to exclude all but Satmars.[22] The answer to this question, which seems to have been assumed by all the members of the court but which was explicitly articulated by Justice Kennedy in his concurring opinion, relies on the same kind of public-private distinction that we saw in *Airmont I*. According to Justice Kennedy:

> the Establishment Clause does not invalidate a town or a state "whose boundaries are derived according to neutral historical and geographic criteria, but whose population *happens* to comprise co-religionists." [citation omitted.] People who share a common religious belief or lifestyle may live together without sacrificing the basic rights of self-governance that all American citizens enjoy, so long as they do not use those rights to establish their religious faith. Religion flourishes in community, and the Establishment Clause must not be construed as some sort of homogenizing solvent that forces unconventional religious groups to choose between assimilating to mainstream American culture or losing their political rights. There is more than a fine line, however, between the *voluntary* association that leads to a political community comprised of people who share a common religious faith, and the forced separation that occurs when the government draws explicit political boundaries on the basis of people's faith.[23] (Emphasis added.)

According to Justice Kennedy, "[i]n creating the Kiryas Joel Village School District, New York crossed that line," but not in creating the village of Kiryas Joel itself.[24] Justice Kennedy's opinion implies that the Village just "happened" to be made up exclusively of Satmars, but that the school district's homogeneous composition was deliberate. This distinction between accidental and intentional religious homogeneity interacts with and presupposes a prior distinction between voluntary (private) associations and public ones.

After all, it could hardly be maintained that the religious character of the territory of Kiryas Joel was accidental, in the sense of a spontaneously occurring (or even more implausibly, *recurring*) phenomenon, beyond human control. The religious character of Kiryas Joel is obviously not a freak accident, but rather something which is actively managed and maintained. But by what mechanism? It is not, and constitutionally could not be, upheld by a village charter, zoning law, or any other official governmental mechanism requiring membership in the Satmar community. Indeed, the Satmars had no need for any such public law of exclusion. Through the exercise of standard rights of private property, individual contract, and the various components of familial and religious control over education and socialization that are constitutionally recognized and protected as "privacy rights," the objective of excluding non-Satmars had already been accomplished prior to the formation of the village.

New York state law, like the law of most states, allows any territorially defined population to incorporate itself as a village so long as it meets certain minimal population and procedural requirements.[25] The Satmars only came to be in a position to form a separate village because a sufficient number of individual members had acquired a set of contiguous lots of private property. As more and more Satmars moved in and purchased properties in the area, more and more non-Satmars moved out, selling to the Satmars as they left. Once enough Satmar families acquired these privately held properties, they could ensure that occupancy would remain exclusively Satmar in the future through a variety of formal and informal "private," albeit collective, controls. On a formal level, private property owners could enter into reciprocal mutually restrictive covenants, pledging not to transfer rights of ownership or occupancy to non-Satmars in the future.[26] Such covenants, which represent a specialized form of contract used in the context of real estate, and which bind successive owners as well as the original parties to the contract, are no different in form from the ubiquitous covenants, conditions, and restrictions standardly employed to give condominium owners and private homeowners associations the power to consent to, veto, or otherwise control new members. They are also no different in form from the racially restrictive covenants that white owners used for decades to keep private property from getting into "non-Caucasian" hands.

The idea that these voluntary agreements do not constitute state action, and that state action forms no part of them, depends upon a highly formalistic distinction between private and state action. On the basis of the public-private distinction, the state, as such, is cleared of any responsibility for religious exclusion that results from their enforcement.[27] According to this mode of reasoning, state officials bear no responsibility for acts of exclusion or self-exclusion that reflect the private preferences of individuals operating in the market for real estate, and in the parallel "marketplace of ideas," in which religious affiliations are supposedly selected. Of course, from a sociological perspective we know that such preferences are not the product of purely voluntary, individual choice but the carefully regulated outcomes of diffuse yet pervasive and powerful processes of socialization, controlled by communal institutions such as families, churches, cultures, and schools. Yet, from the standpoint of the traditional liberal distinction between public and private realms, individual preferences are properly considered to be accidental, that is to say, incidental to the powers of collective regulation that are formally recognized and exercised only in the public realm.

By defining behavioral preferences, like the choice to live "with your own kind," as private factors of individual choice, the public-private distinction obscures the community's reliance on legally protected collective forces of regulation and enforcement. In the case of Kiryas Joel, not only was the Satmar community endowed with considerable power over the socialization of its children; it also exercised significant powers of "private" control regarding the punishment of internal dissenters. Despite the high degree of conformity and cohesion generally exhibited by the community, the decision to establish a Satmar public school in fact provoked strong internal dissent. Dissenters faced severe communal sanctions: social shunning and the denial of access to the village cemetery and places of worship. Such sanctions are enormously powerful, even though they are not directly enforced by official courts of law. Despite the fact that they are not directly enforced by civil legal institutions, the private enforcement of these sanctions does require exercising the rights of private property (in the cemetery and places of worship) which *are* backed by the state's civil authority. The efficacy of these sanctions further depends on the disciplined members' ongoing desire to participate in the community's prescribed cultural and religious practices—a desire induced by the community's constitutionally protected "private" powers of socialization and education. The powers of private punishment themselves play an inestimable role in producing and enforcing the very beliefs, desires, and preferences which make these private sanctions effective. Individual rights of property and choice, communal institutions and practices, and collective sanctions thus form part of a seamless cultural web in which individual beliefs and preferences are produced. From this standpoint, it is sheer folly to try to separate private individual choice from the products of state-backed collective regulation.

Nonetheless, that is exactly what the reasoning of *Kiryas Joel* and *Airmont I* purports to do. Insisting on a formalistic distinction between the public and the private serves a dual function in these cases. On one hand, as already noted, it serves to remove the responsibility for acts of exclusion from state or local government by imputing them to purely private preferences, agreements, and property relations. On the other hand—yet by the same token—the public-private distinction defines the nature of the material basis of a community's means of territorial control in a liberal society. Only by amassing a sufficient amount of *private property* does a community like the Satmars' put itself in a position in which members can exercise their individual rights of political participation in a way that establishes effective local political control. Establishing residence in a particular area is ordinarily a prerequisite for participating in that area's local political elections and other democratic processes.[28] Once enough members of a community have established their private residence, majoritarian procedures of democratic politics more or less ensure either that the existing political jurisdiction will become subject to that community's control, or, alternatively, that the community can secede to form its own local political jurisdiction. Occupying private property is the essential underpinning to political—territorial control in either of these two scenarios. But as long as the formalistic distinction between public power and private rights is maintained, the resulting character (in these cases, the religiously exclusive character) of the political jurisdiction can be regarded as a happenstance.

This is apparently the reasoning that underlies the courts' acceptance of the constitutionality of the villages of *Airmont I* and *Kiryas Joel*. What remains a puzzle, then, is why the Supreme Court nonetheless found the original school district of Kiryas Joel to be unconstitutional, since the religiously exclusive character of the school district's population was no less a happenstance of the private realm than was the homogeneous character of the village. Indeed, the composition of the school district's and the village's populations had to result from precisely the same forces (of private socialization and property relations) because the school district and the village contain the *same* population. It is one and the same community that first established itself in the private precincts of Monroe, then seceded to form the village of Kiryas Joel, and later petitioned the state to form its own school district.

It is true that the Satmar community is required to comply with certain constitutional and legal constraints whenever it exercises its official powers of government (as either a village or a public school). Whereas the private community is permitted to run itself hierarchically, the village and the school district must be run in conformity with the democratic procedures prescribed by state law. (Elections must be held, hearings must be open, and so on.) Similarly, the private institutions of the community are not subject to precisely the same constitutional and statutory prohibitions against discrimination on the basis of race, creed, religion, etc. that bind all governmental entities.[29] Nor are the community's private actions bound by the establishment clause's prohibition against employing governmental power toward religious ends or becoming "entangled" with religion.[30] Under this constitutional prohibition, the village and the school district may pursue "secular" or even "cultural" *but not religious* ends, through secular or cultural *but not religious* means—limitations which do not bind the private religious institutions of the Satmar community.

The distinction between the "religious" and the "secular" drawn under the establishment clause tracks the public-private distinction which we have been discussing, and serves as another essential component of the legal reasoning by which the legitimacy of religiously exclusive local governments is explained. The public domain in which government operates must remain secular; religion is relegated to the private realm. But how are secular/cultural functions distinguished from religious ones? The prevailing liberal legal understanding of the difference between religious and secular/cultural functions clearly differs from ways of conceptualizing the relationship of the sacred to the secular embraced by certain other cultures, including the Hasidic culture. In the conventional liberal view, religion is relegated to the private realm of church and community and, ultimately, to the inner sanctum of the individual conscience.[31] The Satmars' way of understanding the place of the sacred in quotidian life is a perfect illustration of a holistic approach that challenges such a formal or categorical distinction between religious and secular realms. From its inception, Hasidism was based on the notion that the sacred pervades all of life, including the most mundane activities. This is not to say that Hasidic belief systems like the Satmars' lack any notion of the profane. But this is quite different from categorizing activities as intrinsically religious or nonreligious. The conventional liberal designation of political and adjudicative activities as public, and by that token, secular, simply makes no sense from the holistic viewpoint of traditional Judaism, according to which the exposition and application of the law are a quintessentially religious, and at the same time, communal activities.

As a device for identifying which activities are endowed with religious significance for the Satmars, the liberal religious-secular distinction is simply too rigid, asserting bright-line classifications in a cultural context where none is to be found. It imposes a false order, at odds with the reality of the Satmars' experience. In the Satmars' self-understanding, goals such as linguistic separation and cultural self-preservation are inseparable from religious aims.

And yet the conventional liberal distinction between the secular and the religious was essential to the Satmars' defense of the constitutionality of an exclusively Hasidic school district, and they did not hesitate to rely upon it. They attested at length to the "merely cultural" *as opposed to religious* character of the school district, as summarized by the dissenting judges in *Kiryas Joel*:

The school under scrutiny is a public school specifically designed to provide a public secular education to handicapped students. The superintendent, who is not Hasidic, is a 20-year veteran of the New York City public school system, with expertise in the area of bilingual, bicultural, special education. The teachers and therapists at the school all live outside the village of Kiryas Joel. While the village's private schools are profoundly religious and strictly segregated by sex, classes at the public school are co-ed and the curriculum secular. The school building has the bland appearance of a public school, unadorned by religious symbols or markings; and the school complies with the laws and regulations governing all other New York State public schools.[32]

In the same vein, proponents of the school district argued that it was established to accommodate the cultural and psychological—*not* the religious—needs of the community. They asserted that the goal was to spare disabled Satmar children the "emotional trauma" they suffered in the regional public schools from the "additional handicap of cultural distinctiveness."[33] The use of Yiddish in the school was similarly defended as a way to achieve the basic educational goals of bilingual education, rather than religious ends, just as being in the exclusive company of Hasidic children was defended as a way to create a culturally and psychologically comfortable learning environment.

By enabling the community to describe its project as one of cultural rather than religious separatism, the formalistic liberal distinction between secular and religious realms lent essential support to the argument that public officials were not themselves engaged in religious exclusion, or in any other kind of religion-oriented activity. To defend the school district against the charge that it was essentially a religious enterprise, it was not enough to locate the mechanism for excluding non-Satmars in the private realm, for even if the homogeneity of the population is secured through private means, the school district officials that represent that population are still required to comply with the edicts of constitutional law. A formalistic distinction between religious and secular functions makes these requirements relatively easy to satisfy. So long as the community's goals of self-perpetuation and insulation can be described as cultural and secular functions, the public school (and other government) officials can legally implement them.

A similar distinction between religious and nonreligious concerns supported the argument that the village of Airmont was *not* established to implement anti-Semitic policies. Judge Goettel acknowledged that Airmont's "new" zoning code was just a resurrection of Ramapo's old town zoning code, which, the founders of Airmont had complained, was only laxly enforced against the new Jewish arrivals. But, as in Kiryas Joel, local government activities that "happened" to favor or disfavor a certain religion's way of life were deemed to be religiously neutral, so long as they assumed the form of typical secular governmental functions. If Orthodox Jews found that they were guaranteed to be a political minority, predictably unable to prevail in land use regulation disputes after the incorporation of the village of Airmont, that was not due—according to this argument—to any *religious* animosity. It simply reflected the newly carved-out majority's preference for certain patterns of land use over others, a cultural preference, not a religious (or anti-religious) one.

The willingness to accept such a categorical distinction between religiously biased and religiously neutral functions played an obvious role in supporting Judge Goettel's conclusion that Airmont did not disfavor Jews. This distinction played a more subtle role in the Supreme Court's decision in *Kiryas Joel*, which did, after all, rest on the conclusion that the original school district authorization was "substantially equivalent" to a religious establishment. The crucial point here is that this conclusion was *not* based on a rejection of the school district's claim to be serving secular functions. Nor was it based on refuting the basic concept of a bright-line distinction between religious and secular domains. It certainly involved no recognition of the religious significance attributed to mundane activities in the Satmars' worldview. On the contrary, the majority of the Supreme Court tacitly agreed with the dissenting justices' characterization of the "secular" (*ipso facto* non-religious) character of the school. This agreement presupposed the Court's acceptance of the secular-religious distinction, which, in turn, informed its prescription for how to make a religiously homogeneous school district, like the Satmars', constitutional.

Indeed, while striking down the original state act which authorized the creation of Kiryas Joel's Hasidic school district, the Supreme Court provided a virtual blueprint for how to do it again, properly. This blueprint was based upon the conventional liberal view of the distinction between secular and religious realms, in addition to three other conceptual distinctions analyzed throughout this paper (the public-private distinction; the distinction between neutral intentions and neutral effects; and the distinction between formalistic and nonformalistic understandings of particularistic, as opposed to general or universalist, political regimes).

The recipe for a *constitutional* religiously homogeneous public school district (or local governmental institution of any sort) received its most explicit articulation in the concurring opinion of Justice O'Connor. As she noted, "[f]ortunately for the Satmars, New York state law had a way of accommodating their concerns"—to wit, *general* enabling statutes, as opposed to statutes that benefit only one group. The difference between general and special legislation that O'Connor is pointing to here can be illustrated by comparing the form of New York's village incorporation statute, under which the village of Kiryas Joel was constitutionally incorporated, to the constitutionally defective legislation under which the school district was originally formed. The village incorporation act enables *any* community to form a village, so long as it meets certain basic requirements, such as territorial contiguity, minimum population size, and the manifestation of popular consent which have no bearing on the identity of the group. By contrast, the state act that originally authorized the creation of the school district of Kiryas Joel singled out the Satmars' village for the privilege of incorporating its own public school system; no other villages were allowed to form their own school districts under current state law.[34] According to the Supreme Court, it was this particularistic, as opposed to general character, that was constitutionally fatal. But then, as Justice O'Connor explained, in drawing out the implications of the Court's reasoning, there was an obvious remedy:

> There is nothing improper about a legislative intention to accommodate a religious group, so long as it is implemented through generally applicable legislation. New York may, for instance, allow all villages to operate their own school districts. If it does not want to act so broadly, it may set forth neutral criteria that a village must meet to have a school district of its own; these criteria can then be applied by a state agency, and the decision would then be reviewable by the judiciary. A district created under a generally applicable scheme would be acceptable even though it coincides with a village which was consciously created by its voters as an enclave for their religious group.[35]

In other words, if the state would just replace the special legislation, which singled out the village of Kiryas Joel, with general legislation giving all similarly situated village-communities the right to form their own public schools, without regard to their particular group identity, the guarantee given by the establishment clause of no religious favoritism would be satisfied. Not surprisingly, the state of New York lost no time in following Justice O'Connor's explicit advice.

Justice O'Connor's blueprint gave concrete form to an otherwise bewildering general proposition, articulated by Justice Souter, that must have given advocates for the strict separation of church and state cause for grave concern. According to Justice Souter, the Supreme Court does not, in expounding the meaning of the establishment clause, "disable a religiously homogeneous group from exercising political power."[36] Rendered in the affirmative, this means that the constitution, as interpreted and applied by the Supreme Court, *permits* a religiously homogeneous group to exercise political power. One could hardly conceive of a starker contradiction of the truism that liberalism denies holistic communities the capacity for political autonomy and their traditional powers of self-regulation. Indeed, in this context it appears that the very principles of liberalism which are most often assigned the blame for the atomization of community—the bifurcating principles of the public-private and secular-religious distinctions—are the ones that justify state actions that effectively delegate political power to religiously exclusive groups.

Of course, liberal principles, as expounded by Justice Souter and Justice O'Connor, do not justify delegating the powers of government to religiously exclusive communities in every case. *Kiryas Joel* and *Airmont* are, above all, a lesson in the complexity of liberalism. Far from providing blanket approval or disapproval for religiously homogeneous political jurisdictions, these cases suggest a set of principles for distinguishing circumstances in which such jurisdictions satisfy the requirements of liberal state neutrality from circumstances in which they do not. Although the *Kiryas Joel* Court indicated that it would endorse the constitutionality of a *general* village school district enabling statute on grounds similar to those which validated the villages of Airmont and Kiryas Joel, it did, after all, strike down the act which authorized the formation of the school district of Kiryas Joel. Given the Court's acceptance of the secular/nonreligious character of Kiryas Joel's public school, what led it to conclude that the original act was unconstitutional?

Answering this question shows the critical role played by two other conceptual distinctions in the courts' construction of the meaning of official religious neutrality in addition to the more familiar public-private and secular-religious distinctions. What rendered the original act authorizing the Kiryas Joel school district a "religious" establishment in the eyes of the majority was not the *character* of the school's activities, which, the Court agreed were secular, but, rather, the *intentions* behind its formation. In other words, what distinguishes the *legally acceptable* local government institutions that have a decidedly pro- or anti-religious orientation from those that are constitutionally illegitimate (despite their pronounced religious orientation) is the conceptual distinction between government actions that are *intended by the government* to favor or disfavor religion and ones that do so only as an "unintended" effect.

The distinction between intentional, de jure discrimination and unintended, de facto discriminatory effects has had a long and controversial career in the jurisprudence of racial discrimination. Less attention has been paid to the use of the same distinction in the analysis of claims of religious discrimination. Notwithstanding this neglect, *Airmont I* and *Kiryas Joel* exhibit the tendency of some contemporary courts to define the requisite position of state religious neutrality narrowly and formalistically, in terms of this distinction between neutrality of intent and neutrality of effect.

Kiryas Joel provides a clear illustration of how this distinction is applied in the context of religious discrimination claims, and what its practical consequences are. According to the Supreme Court, we recall, the act that was challenged in *Kiryas Joel* was declared unconstitutional because it *intentionally* excluded all but Satmars from the newly drawn jurisdiction, whereas the exclusion of all but Satmars from the village of Kiryas Joel was taken to be, in some jurisprudentially satisfactory sense, accidental. In much the same way, Judge Goettel seems to have regarded the coincidence of Airmont's boundaries and policies with its citizens' "privately" expressed antipathy to "those Jews from Williamsburg" as just that—a coincidence, not a deliberate governmental design. The intent-effect distinction was a key element in the judicial explanation of the legitimacy of the religiously exclusive villages of Airmont and Kiryas Joel.

Clearly, however, there is something odd going on in the legal usage of "intention" when courts are able to maintain, with a straight face, that the exclusion of non-Satmars from the village of Kiryas Joel, and the dilution of the political influence of the "Jews from Williamsburg" in Airmont, were unintentional on the part of political actors who brought the incorporation of these villages about. Only a very technical, specialized usage of the term "intention" could account for the judicial conclusion that drawing the boundary lines around Airmont in a way that *guarantees* the political weakness of the "Jews from Williamsburg" was an accident—or that the homogeneity of Kiryas Joel was an accidental or unintentional effect.

The nature of this technical usage, and its highly formalistic character, cannot be fully understood without further reference to Justice O'Connor's distinction between general (universalist) and group-specific (particularist) legislation. As Justice O'Connor's opinion makes clear, judicial reasoning commonly conflates intentionally biased legislation with group-specific or "special" legislation; conversely, it often equates official neutrality with "general" legislation, that is, legislation that does not single out a particular group, but rather, distributes legal privileges (or disabilities) on a nongroup-specific basis. There is no denying that legislation in the second category may well have the *effect* of advantaging some particular (and even particularistic) groups over others. It may even be that the immediate stimulus to adopting such general legislation is the government's desire to respond to one such particular group. Certainly, no one could deny that this was the case when New York took Justice O'Connor's cue, and passed new legislation enabling all villages to form public school districts at their option. To deny the obvious reality that the new enabling legislation was *intended* by the state to allow the Satmars' school district to continue to exist, in the customary sense of intent, would be the hollowest of formalisms. But Justice O'Connor seems not to be relying on the customary sense of intent. Rather, she implicitly linked the distinction between neutrality of governmental intentions and neutrality of governmental effects to a highly formalistic understanding of the difference between group-specific and general legislation.

It is here that we confront the existence of two competing views of the difference between group-specific and general laws. According to one common view, legislation is group-specific or "particularistic" if it advances the values and objectives of one particular group to the exclusion of others.[37] Particularistic political systems are defined as ones in which members are closely linked by loyalties and obligations to one another, and to the shared heritage and projected future of their group. Political acts are particularistic (in this view) precisely insofar as they reflect a culturally specific belief system, including its conception of morality, its social and political norms, and its criteria of membership. Particularistic governments tend to impose more far-reaching obligations and restrictions on individual members than the merely "negative" (classically liberal) duty to leave other individuals alone. And through the enforcement of such obligations, and of the underlying cultural beliefs and values which these obligations represent, particularistic political systems act to exclude (or at the least, disadvantage) competing value systems. In contrast, governments are nonparticularistic insofar as they refrain from exclusion and bias against competing values, cultures, and beliefs. In short, nonparticularistic governments are inclusive rather than exclusive, internally pluralistic, rather than constituting one of a number of diverse (but internally homogeneous) islands of cultural separatism.

It should be clear that the distinction between general and particularistic legislation implied by the *Kiryas Joel* Court, and enunciated by Justice O'Connor, completely contradicts the way of understanding the distinction which we have just elaborated. Far from inhibiting the establishment of group-specific local government institutions—i.e., local government institutions that advance the aims, and help to perpetuate the existence, of particularistic groups—the *Kiryas Joel* approach to differentiating general from special legislation enables and even encourages the establishment of particularistic municipalities and public schools. Rather than requiring local government units themselves to be nonparticularistic, the Court, in effect, gave particularistic groups both a license and an incentive to establish their own local government institutions. All that is required, according to *Kiryas Joel*'s understanding of the difference between general and particularistic legislation, is that *every* particularistic group be given an equal opportunity to set up its own equally particularistic government institutions. Political separatism, is thus, ironically, re-garded as a form of universalism.

Judge Goettel's reasoning in *Airmont I* relied on a similar equation of equal opportunity, separatism, and nonparticularistic law. In this view, so long as the powers of separate incorporation that permit exclusionary communities to secede are made available to other communities, the government's intent to favor or disfavor a particular community simply does not register as the invidious sort of discriminatory intent prohibited by law. The practical outcome of this sort of reasoning, vividly illustrated by the holding in *Airmont I*, is the legitimation of general village incorporation enabling statutes that permit the establishment of local governments that are, in point of fact, biased against a particular religious group. One might well conclude that it is a highly formalistic conception of nonparticularism that licenses particularistic government in the name of neutral, nonparticularistic, "general" legislation.

We see now how positions that are standardly adopted in liberal legal reasoning can work to exonerate local public institutions that in effect serve to promote the particular ways of life of exclusionary communities. The public-private, the secular-religious, and the intent-effect distinctions, together with the formalistic differentiation between nonparticularistic (neutral) and particularistic (biased) governmental action, permit religiously homogeneous and/or exclusionary communities, legally and in fact, to exercise state-delegated powers of government.

This is not to say that liberal legal reasoning unequivocally endorses this outcome. Liberal thought is not monolithic. It contains within itself competing, and even contradictory, strands of reasoning. Each of the four conceptual distinctions examined above has been subjected to criticism, not only in external critiques of liberalism (e.g., Marxist, communitarian, and conservative critiques), but also in critiques that are internal to liberalism, some of which have been adopted in judicial opinions. In 1948, for example, the Supreme Court issued the important ruling of *Shelley v. Kraemer*, which invalidated the use of racially restrictive covenants by private property owners, on the grounds that they violated the constitutional guarantee of equal protection of the law. In bringing the equal protection clause to bear on private restrictive covenants, the Supreme Court rejected the formalistic distinction between private and state action.[38] And in a 1984 case dealing directly with the conversion of a religious community into a municipality, *Oregon v. City of Rajneeshpuram*, a federal court in Oregon held that the state's recognition of the community's municipal status would constitute the "establishment of a theocracy" because it would *effectively* "confer power on an entity subject to the actual and direct control of a religion and its leaders."[39] In so finding, the court rejected the formalistic distinctions between secular and religious functions, intentionally and accidentally biased effects, and between public and private action asserted in the religious community's defense. Regarding the defendants' claim that "municipal power is in the hands of a body elected according to state law," and therefore has not been "given directly to a religious organization," the Court responded: "Given the . . . control of religious organizations and leaders over all property and all residents in Rajneeshpuram, this distinction may be more formal than substantive." Pursuing this explicitly anti-formalist method of legal analysis, the Oregon court rested its conclusion on the actual *effect* produced by the general state legislation, enabling a religious community to establish its own city, rather than on the intentions behind the general state legislation which "inadvertently" enabled this effect. Refusing to elevate form over substance, the *Rajneeshpuram* court focused on the realities of power relationships within the ostensibly private community, which, in practice, rendered the formal boundary between the private sphere of purely voluntary relations and the public sphere of coercive regulation a fiction.

The conclusion that the establishment clause was *effectively,* albeit not intentionally, violated by the state's recognition of Rajneeshpuram's municipal status could easily be applied to the case of Kiryas Joel—should a court adopt the anti-formalist style of analysis which eschews categorical distinctions between public and private, religious and secular, intentional and accidental matters.[40] Indeed, just such an anti-formalist analysis led to the reversal of *Airmont I* on appeal. Writing for the appellate court in *Airmont II*, Judge Amalya Kearse rejected the formalistic distinctions which undergirded Judge Goettel's conclusion that the *village* of Airmont was not hostile to Orthodox Jews even though its leaders and supporters clearly were, and even though the village was clearly poised to exercise its zoning and other regulatory powers in a manner calculated to thwart the Orthodox way of life. Like *Rajneeshpuram* and *Shelley v. Kraemer, Airmont II* recognizes that the boundary-line between public and private action is unclear. Instead of relying on a formalistic equation between religiously biased state action and *special* legislation that *intentionally* singles out one group, *Airmont II* blurs the distinction between intent and effect by adopting the position that discriminatory intent

> may be inferred from the totality of the circumstances, including the fact, if it is true, that the law bears more heavily on one [group] than another as well as the "historical background of the decision . . . ;" "[t]he specific sequence of events leading up to the challenged decision" . . . ; "contemporary statements by members of the decision-making body" . . . ; and "[s]ubstantive departures."[41]

This style of analysis, which opposes the formalistic distinctions asserted in classical liberal thought, also has a liberal pedigree. Liberalism is a rich and variegated tradition, which provides arguments for and against the proposition that religiously homogeneous communities should be entitled to exercise political power for their own ends. Recognizing this malleability confronts both advocates and critics of Jewish communities like Kiryas Joel with a stark choice: Should they endorse the categorical distinctions of a formalist style of liberal reasoning, which can be deployed in defense of anti-Semitic communities like Airmont, as well as of autonomous Jewish villages like Kiryas Joel? Or should they endorse the anti-formalistic style of analysis, under which both *Airmont* and *Kiryas Joel* stand condemned?

NOTES

1.   A longer version of this essay, which considers the relation of the "formalist" jurisprudence analyzed here to contemporary liberal political theory, in particular, the work of John Rawls and Joseph Raz, appears in *Nomos XXXIX Ethnicity and Group Rights* (N.Y.U. Press) under the title "A Tale of Two Villages (or, Legal Realism Comes to Town)." The author would like to express her gratitude to Tony Lebe, Laura Cadra, and Eugene Sheppard for their helpful assistance.

2.   Factual information about the suburbs of New York described in these pages has been drawn from Elizabeth Lorente, "Haitians in Rockland Back Intervention," *The Bergen Record*, September 15, 1994, A20; Raymond Hernandez, "Storm-Tossed on a Sea of Emotions, New York's Italians Feel Betrayed, Angry and Confused by New Policy on Refugees," *The New York Times*, July 8, 1994, Section B, 1, col.2; Id., "Once a Resort, Village Struggles with Urban Problems," *The New York Times*, June 15, 1994, late edition, Section B, 6, col.1; Ari L. Goldman, "Religion Notes," *The New York Times*, October 9, 1993, late edition, Section 1, 11, col.1.

3.   Ari L. Goldman, "Religion Notes," *The New York Times*, October 9, 1993, A11.

4.   *Board of Education of Kiryas Joel v. Grumet*, 114 S.Ct. 2481 (1994).

5.   *U.S. v. Village of Airmont*, 839 F. Supp. 1054 (S.D.N.Y. 1993) (referred to here as *Airmont I*), rev'd, 67 F. 3d 412 (2d Cir. 1995) (referred to here as *Airmont II*).

6.   See e.g., in the *Matter of North Shore Hebrew Academy v. Leonard S. Wegman*, 105 A.D. 2d 702 (1984); *Jewish Reconstructionist Synagogue of the N. Shore Inc. v. Incorporated Village of Roslyn Harbor* 352 N.E. 2d 115 (N.Y. 1976).

7.   *Board of Education of Kiryas Joel v. Grumet*, 114 S.Ct. 2481, 2585 (1994).

8.   Jerome R. Mintz, *Hasidic People: A Place in the New World* (1992) 51.

9.   *LeBlanc-Sternberg v. Fletcher*, 67 F. 3d 412, 418–19 (2d Cir. 1995).

10. *U.S. v. Village of Airmont*, 839 F. Supp. 1054, 1062–63 (S.D.N.Y. 1993).

11. Id., at 1061.

12. Id., at 1064.

13. See Chapter 748 of the 1989 New York Session Laws.

14. See 114 S.Ct. at 2485.

15. *Board of Education of Kiryas Joel v. Grumet*, at 2484–85 (1994).

16. This principle was established in the previous U.S. Supreme Court decisions, *School Dist. of Grand Rapids v. Ball*, 473 U.S. 373 (1985) and *Aguilar v. Felton*, 473 U.S. 402 (1985).

17. Linda Greenhouse, "The Supreme Court: The Decision," *The New York Times*, June 28, 1994, A14; Associated Press, *Chicago Tribune*, June 27, 1994, C1; David G. Savage, "High Court Upholds Church-State Split," *The Los Angeles Times*, June 28, 1994, A14.

18. For a discussion of the growing controversy over whether the establishment clause is properly interpreted as implicitly incorporating the principle of separation between Church and State see "Development in the Law—Religion and State," 100 *Harvard Law Review*, at 1609, 1633 (1987).

19. *Kiryas Joel*, 114 S.Ct. at 2484.

20. Id., at 2489.

21. Id., at 2490.

22. Non-Satmar "[n]eighbors who did not wish to secede with the Satmars objected strenuously [to being included] and after arduous negotiations the proposed boundaries of the village of Kiryas Joel were drawn to include just the 320 acres owned and inhabited entirely by the Satmars." Id., at 2485. When the boundaries of the village were originally drawn by the state they included some non-Satmars, but they were redrawn to exclude them. Jeffrey Rosen, "Village People," *The New Republic*, April 4, 1994, 11.

23. *Board of Education of Kiryas Joel v. Grumet*, 114 S.Ct. 2481, 2504–05 (1994) (Kennedy, J., concurring). Id., at 2505.

24. Id., at 2505.

25. "[The] right [to form a new village within a town is one] that New York's Village Law gives almost any group of residents who satisfy certain procedural niceties." *Kiryas Joel*, 114 S.Ct. at 2485. (*citing* N.Y. Village Law, Art.2 {McKinney 1973 and Supp. 1994}).

26. In his article in *The New Republic*, Jeffrey Rosen asserts that the community established numerous restrictive housing policies, including (1) the requirement that "anyone who wants to build within its borders pay a tithe of $10,000 to Congregation Yetev Lev"; (2) a prohibition against selling or renting to a new resident without receiving written permission in advance; and (3) a requirement that new residents "sign a contract promising 'to be guided by the laws and ways of the Grand Rabbi' [and] 'only to go to the synagogues under the control of our congregation' and to send their children 'only to the school of Torah Veyreh, and Bais Rachel, that was founded and built by the Grand Rabbi (Joel) and is under the control of the present Rabbi (Moses).'" Rosen, *supra* note 22, 11.

27. In *Shelley v. Kraemer*, 334 U.S. 1 (1948), the Supreme Court held that the enforcement of *racially* restrictive property covenants is unconstitutional on the basis of an anti-formalistic mode of reasoning. In particular, *Shelley v. Kraemer* rejected the formalistic distinction between private discrimination and state enforcement of laws which allow discriminatory action in holding that when a consummated contract of sale between willing buyers and willing sellers is thwarted due to the "active intervention of the state courts, supported by the full panoply of state power," it is absolutely clear that state action has occurred. According to *Shelley* judicial action enforcing private rights "bears the clear and unmistakable imprimatur of the State." Id., at 19–20. However, the court has never addressed the applicability of *Shelley* to religiously restrictive covenants.

28. Scholars have explained that a "state or municipality may restrict the franchise to its bona fide residents." Laurence Tribe, *American Constitutional Law*, (2nd ed. 1988) at 1088–89, (discussing *Dunn v. Blumstein*, 405 U.S. 330, 334, 1972); Pope v. Williams, 193 U.S. 621 (1904).

29. The Fair Housing Act of 1968's strict prohibitions against discrimination in sale or rental of housing based on race, color, sex, familial status, or national origin, do apply to private as well as public actors. However, exemptions are allowed for religious organizations and private clubs as well as for individual

owners of not more than three single family houses, who do not rely on the services of any broker, agent, or sales person. Fair Housing Act of 1968 803, 42 U.S.C. 3603, 3607 (1994).

30. Tribe, *supra* note 28, 1226–27.

31. The Hasidic conceptual system comprehends a distinction between religious and secular affairs but conceives of the two as interrelated parts of the whole rather than as separate, distinct entities. The distinction is typically described by the Satmar (in Yiddish) as one between *yiddishkeit* (Jewishness) and *mentschlichkeit* (humanness). Israel Rubin, *Satmar: An Island in the City* (Chicago, 1972) 103. The distinction between *yiddishkeit* and *mentschlichkeit* refers less to a difference between religious or sacred, and nonreligious or profane affairs, than to the separation between Jewish and non-Jewish realms.

As for the Hasidic conception of the sacred and the profane within the domain of *yiddishkeit*, it has more of the character of a dialectical relationship than that of a sharp distinction between two fixed realms. For example, a central theological concept of Hasidism is that of *avodah be-gashmiyut* (worship through corporeality), which "call[s] for man's worship of God by means of his physical acts," such as "eating, drinking and sexual relations." *Encyclopedia Judaica* (Jerusalem, 1971) 7: 1407. According to this doctrine, matter is transformed into spirit, the profane is transformed into the holy, through communal worship centered around the figure of the *Rebbe* or *zaddik*, as the charismatic leader is also called. But—and this is a critical point in refuting the translation of Hasidic concepts into the English terms of "secular" and "religious"—"[t]hose who surround the *zaddik* are incapable of individually discerning the moment in which the transformation of secular into holy occurs." Id., 1408. As a result, it is impossible to assign any particular human activity or experience into one domain or another, categorically, or even to separate the two domains, either practically or conceptually.

32. *Board of Education of Kiryas Joel v. Grumet*, 114 S.Ct. 2481, 2506 (1994) (Scalia, J., dissenting).

33. Id., at 2509 (Scalia, J., dissenting).

34. Id., at 2498 (O'Connor, J., concurring).

35. Id., at 2498 (O'Connor, J., concurring).

36. Id., at 2493.

37. A compelling articulation of this view of particularism, in contrast to universalism (and of the complexities of the contrast), is contained in Robert M. Cover, "The Supreme Court, 1982 Term—Forward: Nomos and Narrative," 97 *Harvard Law Review* 4 (1983).

38. See note 27 above.

39. *Oregon v. City of Rajneeshpuram*, 598 F. Supp. 1217 (U.S.D.C., District of Oregon, 1984).

40. After this essay was written, the state legislation newly authorizing the Kiryas Joel school district was challenged in *Grumet v. Cuomo*, and found to be unconstitutional, on the basis of precisely the sort of anti-formalist style of analysis exhibited in *Airmont II*, and argued for above.

41. *Airmont II*, 67 F.3d at 425 (quoting *Washington v. Davis*, 426 U.S. 229, 242 (1976) and *United States v. Yonkers Board of Education*, 837 F.2d 1181, 1221 (2d Cir. 1987).

COMMUNAL RITES: THE PUBLIC CULTURE OF AMERICAN JEWS

Arthur Aryeh Goren

Emancipation meant losses as well as gains for Jewry. . . .
Political equality also meant the dissolution of the autonomous
communal organization: the Jews were no longer to be a nation
within a nation. . . . Eventually, it was hoped his [the Jew's]
assimilation would be complete.

Salo Baron, "Ghetto and Emancipation"[1]

In his landmark essay "Ghetto and Emancipation," Salo Baron called for a revision of the prevailing view of the radical break in Jewish history wrought by emancipation. Baron challenged the widespread historiographical perspective that contrasted the "wretchedness" of ghetto existence during the Medieval period with the "Golden Age" ushered in by emancipation. Both images were distorted representations of the historical truth. For instance, modernity did not herald a "new age of liberty and enlightenment." Rather, it transformed "the living Jewish ethnic organism," forcing it "to be pared down to the fiction of the Jewish 'Confession.'" In enlightened Europe, "assimilation via Reform was the Jewish destiny." And yet, Baron observed, complete assimilation had not followed. The chief task of the current and future generations, he concluded, was to assure that the democratic state reach an accommodation—achieve "harmony and balance"—between the individual rights of its minority citizens and "the special minority rights" the group thinks necessary "to protect its living national organism from destruction and absorption by the majority."[2]

Writing in 1928, two years after arriving in the United States, Baron's terse remarks on the future course of Jewish communal life

109

reflected his European biases, fears, and hopes. Nevertheless, his definition of the problem—how to maintain a viable communal order without benefit of formal corporate status—was a pivotal one for American Jewry. As European conditions deteriorated and he became familiar with the dynamics of American Jewish life, Baron changed his views. He lauded "the amazing record of the American Jewish community," attained by a multitude of associations functioning solely on the principle of voluntarism. Given America's open society, nothing prevented Jews from leaving the community either by conscious intent or apathetic drift. For Baron, the American Jewish community offered an alternative model to the European Jewish polities where the vestiges of a state church tradition, a premodern corporatist order, and new political exigencies invested them with a quasi-official status. American Jewry depended upon "communal organisms [that were] entirely optional"; communal membership was determined "by choice" rather than civil regulation. Baron admitted when he made these observations in 1942 that about half of American Jewry did not participate in any organized form of Jewish communal life. But those who did brought a "superior vitality" to their "optional organizations," superior, that is, to those organizations [as in Europe] composed of largely indifferent or unwilling taxpayers.[3]

In fact, this pattern of voluntary associationalism was a fixed feature of American democratic practice with its preference for individual civic initiative over governmental intervention, as well as separation of church and state. The basic law of the land ignored the ethnic and religious realms and left those spheres to the church, fraternal, educational, patriotic, and charitable societies which proliferated in a latitudinarian milieu. Jews found the American model of voluntarism especially compatible to their condition. It best served the need of a heterogeneous population drawn from different countries, possessing a variety of religious customs, divided by class and degrees of acculturation, and, by the early 1900s, further fragmented by secular ideologies. However, taken together, the scores of congregations, social service agencies, national movements, fraternal orders, and educational and recreational centers began to develop a common "culture of organizations." What one observer writing in 1964 noted as characteristic of his times applied, in large measure, to an earlier period as well: "To be a Jew is to belong to an organization. To manifest Jewish culture is to carry out, individually or collectively, the program of an organization"; to attend meetings, raise funds, and listen to speeches is "the Jewish way of life."

To be sure, faced with extraordinary challenges, American Jewry seized on the associationalist impulse, creating such agencies as the Joint Distribution Committee to aid European Jewry and federations of Jewish philanthropies to coordinate local charities.[4]

Alongside this organizational mosaic with its ideology of "acts and tasks, of belonging and conforming," another less-defined domain of Jewish communal life existed, the domain of the public culture of American Jews. It expressed itself in a series of great communal observances. Beginning in the early years of the twentieth century and extending to our times, tens of thousands and sometimes hundreds of thousands of Jews participated in mass meetings, marched in parades, and attended pageants to commemorate, celebrate, or protest events that were of great importance to the Jewish public. The observances were in part civic rituals of affirmation and self-definition, and in part ideological and political statements in the guise of ethnic pageantry. They provided opportunities for transcending the immense class and cultural disparities that divided Jews in the United States at the beginning of the century. Both the medium and the message of these public events were deliberately crafted to attract great numbers, new settlers no less than older ones, the unaffiliated as well as the affiliated. These mass affairs were appeals to "the community" at large even though their sponsors were often party people with partisan designs or representatives of a limited segment of the organized community. These events were clearly intended to exert an impact beyond the Jewish public. The celebratory events took place in the city's main streets, public squares, concert halls, and sports arenas so that the press and non-Jews would also take notice. Indeed, much about these affairs had to do with securing a respected place for American Jews in the civic life of the nation. Communal convocations such as the funeral of Sholom Aleichem, the beloved Yiddish writer who died in New York in 1916, the mass meetings held across the nation in 1933 to protest Nazis atrocities, the political pageants beginning with "The Romance of a People" which was staged at the Chicago World's Fair in 1933, and the year-long celebration of the tercentennial of the founding of the first Jewish settlement in America beginning in 1954, suggest the configuration of that public culture.[5]

The present essay examines three mass events that occurred over a span of eight days during November and early December 1905. Taken together, they offer a paradigm of the public culture of American Jews. Two of these events were commemorated throughout the United States;

the third occurred in New York City alone. The first in time was the funeral of the popular Yiddish novelist and dramatist, Nahum Meyer Shaikevich (better known by his pseudonym, Shomer), which was held on November 26. Nearly 100,000 turned out to honor the writer, lining the funeral route and following the hearse through the streets of New York's Lower East Side and across the Williamsburg Bridge to Union Hills Cemetery in Brooklyn. Four days later, on Thanksgiving Day, in scores of public meetings and synagogues across the land, American Jews celebrated the 250th anniversary of Jewish settlement in America. Governors, mayors, and former U.S. president Grover H. Cleveland participated in the festivities. The celebrations were followed on December 4 with protest demonstrations mourning the victims of the October pogroms in Czarist Russia. Two hundred thousand participated in the New York protest march alone, with more modest demonstrations occurring in other cities and special memorial services held in Jewish communities throughout the U.S.

Of the three events, the funeral of Shaikevich (Shomer) represented the most traditional expression of communal celebration. One can indeed argue that in traditional European Jewish society the public funeral of an illustrious scholar or communal leader was the most significant event in the life of the community. It was a time not only of mourning but of rededication, uplift, and communal solidarity. All who could accompanied the remains of the revered figure to the cemetery. Each detail of the ritual was charged with meaning: those chosen to maintain the final vigil, carry the coffin, and deliver the eulogies; the public places where the procession paused for prayers; and at the cemetery, the location of the grave itself. The orchestration of the funeral ranked and classified the deceased among the community's worthies who had gone to their reward. In the popular mind, the ultimate indicator of esteem was the size of the crowd that accompanied the deceased to the grave. Though secularization breached the walls of the traditional, organic Jewish community of Eastern Europe, and the passage to America reduced them further, the need to rally around the death of a distinguished person in a communal act of solidarity and contrition remained intact. Time-honored religious custom still resonated in freethinking America.[6]

Shomer, who came to the United States in 1889 with a considerable reputation, had made his name as the most prolific writer of his time. The author of more than two hundred novels and scores of plays (many of both genre adapted and popularized from the works of others),

Shomer was the master of what we would call today low-brow literature. (His critics, among them Sholom Aleichem, called him the "father of *shund*," literary trash.) His was a popular, accessible literature, and the masses soaked up its social messages and stirring historical tales of Jewish heroism. Typical of the former was *Der yidisher poritz* (*The Jewish Mogul*), a novel Shomer later adapted for the stage, which was a devastating portrayal of the fanaticism, imperiousness, and arid piety of the shtetl autocracy. An example of the latter was *Der letzer yidisher kenig* (*The Last Jewish King*), a drama of the Bar Kochba-led revolt against the Romans. Shomer's collaboration with the pioneers of the Yiddish theater began in Europe, and continued in New York, where his plays on immigrant life and current affairs became staples of the Yiddish stage. His novels were serialized in the *Morgn zhurnal* and *Tageblat*. David Blaustein, the director of the Educational Alliance, recalled reading Shomer's novels as a young boy: "I was one of many who was started on the road to culture (*Bildung*) by Shomer's writings." When Shomer died, the Jewish immigrant quarter responded in the traditional way to the call to honor an important figure—a writer and teacher of the people, or a great *maggid*, a beloved preacher.[7]

Yet who in fact determined the degree of honors Shomer should receive? Who planned the funeral, chose the honorees, the eulogists, the order of march, the procession's route? In short, who defined the community's character and its self-image? In European towns where the traditional community structure was still in place, the *kehillah* leadership, including its rabbis and learned men, made these determinations. Where the traditional leadership was challenged, an unresolved struggle for hegemony ensued. In New York, the Yiddish press decided, a press that spoke for distinct ideological camps. The day of Shomer's death (a Friday, which allowed more time for preparations, since the funeral could not be held until after the Sabbath), the publishers of the Yiddish dailies met at the Educational Alliance, the uptown-supported social and cultural center of the immigrant quarter. All Yiddish journalists, artists and intellectuals (*maskilim*), the publishers resolved, should join in making the funeral a "general one," that is, nonpartisan, and urge all Jews of New York to take part. Jacob Saphirstein, the publisher of the politically conservative and religiously Orthodox *Morgn zhurnal*, and David Blaustein of the Educational Alliance were charged with making the arrangements. To advise them, an executive committee of two representatives of each paper was appointed. The Educational Alliance was chosen for the memorial meeting. The proprietors of the Yiddish theaters, the various actors' unions and their chorus, and the typesetters union announced that they would come in organized contingents, and the choristers volunteered to sing at the services.[8]

For three days, the conservative *Tageblat* and *Morgn zhurnal*, and the socialist *Varhayt* and *Forverts* sang Shomer's praises. The *Forverts*, a harsh critic of Shomer in the past, remarked: "Whatever one might say of the literary worth of his works, they were of great value for a large part of the Jewish people. Through Shomer's novels many thousands learned to read." Furthermore, he had imbued them with a thirst for *Bildung*—education, culture, self-improvement. The *Forverts*, like the other papers, urged all classes to attend and outlined the funeral route.[9]

In reporting the funeral, the Yiddish press struck an inspirational and ecumenical note. The *Tageblat* began its account: "Where else can one find a city like New York and where else can one find such Jews as in New York. In no country, and in no city, and at no time in history has one witnessed such an exalted expression of *Judenthum* (Jewishness) as at Shomer's funeral." The *Forverts* proclaimed: "Young and old, religious and freethinkers, Jews of all hues and types came to honor and accompany the deceased to the grave." The *Tageblat* estimated that at least a hundred thousand crowded into the side streets near the Educational Alliance and along the route of the cortege.[10] As the hearse traversed the East Side, *The New York Times* reported, "Jacob P. Adler, the tragedian," walked to the left of the hearse and by his side Saphirstein of the *Morgn zhurnal*. At each synagogue along the way "the procession stopped and the rabbi and congregants came out and sang a hymn for the dead."[11]

Traditional in form, the funeral was arranged with great care. The planners stressed inclusiveness and aesthetics, taking into account both the sensibilities of the acculturating, "modern" Jews and the curiosity of non-Jewish observers. The arrangements committee announced through the Yiddish press that notables and family friends wishing to pay their respects prior to the funeral should appear at the Educational Alliance for an identity button allowing them into the Shomer home. At the appointed time, writers, actors, and representatives of the theater and typesetters unions carried the coffin to the hearse, and a combined choir of the Yiddish theaters, chanting psalms, marched before the hearse over the short distance to the Educational Alliance. Admission to the memorial service was by invitation only. The list of eulogists represented the range of Jewish political and cultural life: Adolf Radin, rabbi of the Alliance's People's Synagogue (who spoke in German), David Blaustein, the Alliance's director, socialist Abe Cahan of the *Forverts*, John Paley of the *Tageblat*, Joseph Barondess, Zionist leader and radical, Boris Thomashafsky, the actor and stage director, and the Orthodox preacher, Hirsh Tsvi Masliansky. Between speeches the theater choristers alternated with the downtown cantors' choir in chanting psalms from the funeral service. The renowned downtown cantor, Pinkhas Minkovsy, concluded the service with the memorial prayer, *El male rahamim.* All of the accounts stressed the sense of exaltation that permeated the meeting and the perfect order that marked the procession.[12]

In its editorial the day of the funeral, the *Tageblat* offered some interesting reflections on the event's wider significance. The column was subtitled: "The Future City of Historical Jewish Funerals." Shomer's funeral, the paper predicted, would be the third funeral of historic proportions that New York Jews had participated in, if size and feelings were the criteria. First had come the unforgettable mass funeral in 1902 of Jacob Joseph, the eminent Vilna preacher who was invited to serve as "chief rabbi" in the abortive experiment to strengthen the communal life of New York's Orthodox Jews. At least 100,000 took part. And in January, 1905, Kasriel Sarasohn, publisher of the *Tageblat* and patron of downtown charities, was similarly honored. In both cases, not only the Yiddish but the general press gave detailed coverage in laudatory, even reverential, terms. And now, all within a mere three years, the third historic funeral was about to begin. "In no other city in the world," the *Tageblat* declared,

> have there been such grand funerals. Our generation and the next to come will have the task of rendering final tributes to the illustrious figures of the Jewish world when their time will come to take leave. New York is at present the greatest Jewish center in the world. Within the next five years all the distinguished Jews in Russia will have settled among us.[13]

During the lifetime of the immigrant generation, religious, cultural, and political associations organized funeral pageants for their luminaries, providing the Jewish public for a moment with a sense of uplift and communal solidarity. For instance, the funeral of the great Yiddish humorist, Sholom Aleichem, in May 1916 brought 250,000 Jews into the streets, with the New York Kehillah (aspiring to be the coordinating agency of the Jewish community) planning and directing the ceremony with the essential help of the Yiddish press. Conducted with the grandeur of a Jewish state funeral, the procession passed through three New York boroughs, pausing before representative Jewish institutions for memorial prayers and eulogies, and attracting Jews from all ranks and circles. In expressing their affection for their beloved cultural hero, Jews were also demonstrating their solidarity with the "old home" Sholom Aleichem wrote about, which was now ravaged by war.[14]

If the funeral marked an important manifestation of American Jewish public culture, a commemorative event of a different order was the celebration of the 250th anniversary of the first Jewish settlement on the North American continent. In 1654, twenty-three Jews arrived in New Amsterdam aboard the *Sainte Catherine*, expelled from the Dutch colony of Recife in Brazil after its conquest by the Portuguese. The proposal to commemorate the establishment of the first settlement originated among the elitist circles of the established Jewish community. Their intention was to enshrine the event—heretofore hardly noticed, let alone celebrated—in the nation's pantheon of founding myths. Turning the anniversary into a nationwide commemoration offered a superb opportunity to achieve several goals: prove the venerable lineage of America's Jews; reiterate once more the presumed affinity of Americanism and Judaism; and have others—mainly the non-Jewish notables and newspaper editorialists—praise both the rectitude and civic virtues of the Jews and their material and cultural contributions to the nation.[15]

Historians have sought to explain the mindset of the planners, who were primarily of German origin, as stemming from the conflicted soul of the ambitious and insecure. Eminently successful in business and the professions, fervently American and yet craving acceptance, they faced the impediment of a pervasive prejudice. They were barred from the proper clubs, boards of trustees, and philanthropies; their children were blocked from attending the desired private schools; their sons and daughters were excluded from some colleges and from the better fraternities; and they suffered from the intellectual anti-Semitism common in literary and academic circles. To add to their disquiet, like a plague from Egypt came the Jews from Russia. Their co-religionists' startling distinctiveness and their dire poverty made the responsibilities that kinship imposed especially burdensome—an obstacle in the pursuit of social inclusion. Understandably, the Jewish elite became preoccupied with a dignified refutation of those antisemitic canards of parasitism and disloyalty that were cast upon them.[16]

There was also a more sanguine face to the importance assigned by Americanized Jews to the 250th anniversary. An authentic interest in historical roots and processes was astir in America. Kindled by an energetic secularizing nationalism sometime in the 1870s, Americans began celebrating their past with unprecedented zeal. History became the medium for defining their national identity and glorifying what they perceived to be the moral superiority of the Republic. On a local level, commemoration of the anniversaries of Revolutionary War battles, Civil War heroes, and pioneer settlements became widespread. Cities observed the bicentennial or centennial of their founding in festivities that sometimes lasted as long as a week. Nationally, the Centennial Exposition of American Independence held at Philadelphia in 1876 and the 1893 Columbian Exposition in Chicago stand out. One of the most patrician expressions of this phenomenon, initiated by the first professionally trained historians (the new guardians of the past), was the formation of the American Historical Association in 1884. Dedicated to a "scientific" reconstruction of the past, the association drew to its ranks Brahmin amateur practitioners as well as the new breed of university-trained historians.[17]

Six years later the American Jewish Historical Society (AJHS) was established for some of the same reasons by a similar mix of professionals and interested patricians. At the first "scientific meeting" of the society, founding president Oscar Straus, scion of the great mercantile family and author of a book on Old Testament influences on the origins of republican government in America, declared: "The objects of our Society . . . are not *sectarian*, but American—to throw an additional ray of light upon the discovery, colonization, and history of our country." For Straus, that "additional ray of light"—the exploration of the part Jews played in the early settlement of the colonies—was a way not only of contributing "to the general history of our country" but of uncovering for Americans and Jews the authentic identity of American Jewry. Straus and others among the AJHS founders would play a central role in the 250th anniversary celebration.[18]

Among America's ethnic groups, Jews were not alone in displaying a self-consciousness and assertiveness that developed in tandem with the nation's intensified reverence for its past. Ethnic associations participated in the local celebrations, marching in the parades dressed in their ethnic costumes and often mounting historical floats. At the Philadelphia Centennial Exposition, six ethnic and religious groups had their "days"—a parade culminating in the unveiling of a monument on the fairground. The Jewish monument, commissioned by the B'nai B'rith and executed by the American Jewish sculptor Moses Ezekiel, represented "religious freedom:" "The statue of a woman, symbolizing religious liberty, dominates the monument, her right arm sheltering a boy holding a flaming lamp representing faith in a higher power, her left arm pointing to the scroll of the constitution." Interestingly, the German, Irish, Italian, and African-American monuments depicted ethnic heroes: Wilhelm Humboldt, Father Matthew (an Irish temperance advocate), Christopher Columbus, and Richard Allen (an ex-slave who founded the African Methodist Episcopal Church).[19]

Perhaps the most impressive ethnic commemorations prior to the 250th American Jewish celebration was the German-American celebrations of 1883. Marking the bicentennial of the founding of Germantown, Pennsylvania, by thirteen families from the Rheinish town of Krefeld, German cultural and social associations staged impressive pageants in the major centers of German-American population. The central feature of the day was the parade which included floats depicting the history of German-Americans—the founding of Germantown, German participation in America's wars, and German-American economic contributions—in addition to marching rifle companies and bands. (In a number of cities, the 1883 bicentennial inaugurated an annual "German Day.") Five years later Swedes, concentrated in the Midwest, celebrated the 250th anniversary of the founding of the first Swedish settlement at Fort Christina on the Delaware River. In both cases, tentative steps were taken to establish historical societies. In this way, ethnic Americans promoted their own founding myths, insisting on equality of place.[20]

In February 1905, the proposal to observe the 250th anniversary of Jewish settlement on a nationwide scale was broached by two separate bodies: New York's Sephardic Congregation Shearith Israel (the oldest Jewish congregation in the United States) and the American Jewish Historical Society at its annual conference. By spring, a joint ad hoc committee had appointed an executive committee to direct "the Committees in Charge of the General Celebration." The executive committee, a mix of wealth and intellect, was headed by the bankers Jacob Schiff (chairman), and Isaac N. Seligman (treasurer) and included other leading establishment personages such as Cyrus Adler, Daniel Guggenheim, Adolph Lewisohn, Louis Marshall, Oscar Straus, and Judge Mayer Sulzberger. All of the states as well as Alaska, Puerto Rico, and the Indian Territory were represented on the two–hundred member general committee which was apparently a purely honorary body. No Russian Jews served on the executive committee, though eight Russian Jews, including the editors of the Yiddish dailies and several prominent rabbis, were appointed to the general committee.[21]

The executive committee chose Thanksgiving Day as the appropriate occasion for the celebration, and launched an educational campaign to make Jews conscious of their American origins. Lecturers spoke on the topic and lengthy articles appeared with regularity in the Anglo-Jewish press. In early May the Anglo-Jewish press published long excerpts from papers delivered at a meeting of the "Judaeans," a social-literary society of the New York Jewish elite. In June, the Boston [Jewish] *Advocate* reported on the first of a series of celebrations that would continue until the "general celebration" on Thanksgiving Day. In the issue of the *Advocate* that appeared following the 4th of July, the lead banner read: "On Thanksgiving-Day next, the Hebrew Communities of the United States will commemorate fittingly the 250th anniversary of the arrival of their Pilgrim Fathers," and readers were informed that the Boston committee had chosen Faneuil Hall, "the cradle of liberty," as the site of the Thanksgiving Day convocation.[22]

In a widely reprinted lecture, Louis Marshall captured the mixture of apologetics and self-assertiveness that became the leitmotif of the anniversary:

> It has been a popular fallacy, that the Jew has been a latecomer on American soil; that he has been unwilling to undergo the hardships of the pioneer, or to create new paths for industry and commerce; that his admittance within our gates has been a matter of grace and bounty, and that his rights are inferior in antiquity to those of our population who have other racial and religious affinities. But when we remember that the settlement at Jamestown, Virginia, was in 1607, that of the Dutch at New Amsterdam in 1614, that of Pilgrims at Plymouth Rock in 1620 and that the first settlement of the Jews in New York occurred in 1655, the latter are to be regarded as of equal rank with the most ancient American settlers.[23]

In October, the committee distributed a pamphlet, "Notes Relating to the Celebration," which included guidelines for observing the approaching jubilee. Congregations were instructed to hold special services on the Saturday or Sunday preceding Thanksgiving Day, and an "Order of

Service" for that Sabbath was attached. The service was prepared by a committee of eminent rabbis representing the major denominations that included the Orthodox Dr. H. Pereira Mendes, the Conservative Professor Solomon Schechter, head of the Jewish Theological Seminary, and Reform's Dr. Kaufman Kohler, head of the Hebrew Union College. A reprint of Cyrus Adler's history of the Jews in America from the recently published *Jewish Encyclopedia* and an annotated bibliography were included. In addition, long accounts of the history of American Jews were featured in major newspapers and periodicals.[24]

November was not a good month for festivities. Details of the death and devastation of the October pogroms in Russia (400 Jews were killed in Odessa alone), and further outbreaks in the first week of November propelled the established community as well as the immigrant community to an unprecedented outburst of activity. Relief committees were formed, protest meetings held, and memorial services called. Under these circumstances, some communities—Chicago, Milwaukee, Cincinnati, Philadelphia—abandoned plans for mass celebrations. The national anniversary committee announced that the subscriptions it had solicited for a memorial statue to mark the 250th anniversary would now be directed "to the immediate relief of the distress of our unfortunate brethren there." However, despite the pall of the pogroms, the national committee went ahead with the central event of the country-wide celebration, which took place in New York's Carnegie Hall.[25]

The "great celebration" in Carnegie Hall, *The Times* reported, "resolved itself into a demonstration likely to become historic in the annals of that famous meeting place." The setting was indeed an august one. The exercises began with the honored guests and members of the executive committee led by Jacob Schiff marching into the hall single file to the strains of Mendelssohn's "March of the Priests" from *Athalie* played by the New York Symphony Orchestra. To the thunderous applause of a packed house of 5,000, the dignitaries took their places on a stage already crowded with the People's Choral Union and the Downtown Cantors' Association. The lavish decor of the hall added to the majesty of the occasion. The lower boxes were draped in bright red decorated with the coats of arms of the different states; green hangings "embossed with golden bucklers emblematic of Jerusalem," according to *The Times*, adorned the second tier; and "festoons of American flags" bedecked the galleries and stage. Befitting the aura of an affair of state, a letter from President Theodore Roosevelt was read, while the speakers included ex-president Grover Cleveland, Governor Frank Higgins of

New York, and New York City's mayor, George B. McClellan. The committee had chosen the other speakers with a shrewd diplomatic eye. Temple Emanuel's rabbi opened the meeting and Shearith Israel's rabbi closed it; the Episcopal Bishop of New York spoke; and the "oration" was delivered by Judge Mayer Sulzberger of Philadelphia, a rising figure in Jewish communal life and a Jewish scholar of some breadth. The capstone of the musical program—the program itself included choruses from Mendelssohn's *Elijah* and Bruch's *Kol Nidre*—was the singing of "Adon Olam" by the Downtown Cantors. "The solemn hymn," *The Times* remarked, "was beautifully sung. . . . Their voices would have done credit to the Metropolitan Opera House." For the planners, the cantors constituted the immigrant presence in the ecumenical homage to the Jews of America.[26]

Two of the recurring themes in the anniversary addresses deserve special attention. The first linked the twenty-three Jews who had landed in New Amsterdam in 1654 on the *Sainte Catherine* to the band of Pilgrims who had arrived at Plymouth Rock on the *Mayflower* thirty-four years earlier. In impressive historical detail, speaker after speaker spun out the remarkable interlocking fate of Pilgrim and Jew. Persecuted and hunted because of their religious faith, both had found haven in tolerant Holland. Soon after the Pilgrims left for the New World, the Jews left Holland for the Dutch colonies in Brazil and, when expelled by the Portuguese, found refuge in New Amsterdam. Philadelphia's Rabbi Joseph Krauskopf declared (in words echoed by other orators): "Within the cabins of the *Mayflower* and the *Sainte Catherina* were those principles conceived that gave birth to the battle cry of 1776." Oscar Straus embellished the Pilgrim/Puritan-Jewish-Dutch connection by pointing out that at the very time that the Dutch West Indies Company deliberated over the petition to grant Jews leave to remain in New Amsterdam, Rabbi Menasseh Ben Israel of Amsterdam met with Oliver Cromwell to negotiate the resettlement of the Jews in England. Among the supporters of readmission was Roger Williams, founder of the colony of Rhode Island and defender of religious liberty ("Soul-freedom"), who was completing a stay in London on the eve of the negotiations. Thus, Straus and his fellow speakers stressed, from America's earliest history, the Jews were linked with the champions of religious liberty.[27]

"Columbus," the other motif, provided two inspiring images. Speakers cited historians and quoted sources that coupled the launching of Columbus' expedition with the expulsion of the Jews from Spain. As

Columbus sailed out of the harbor of Palos with his little fleet to discover the New World, the audiences were told, he passed ships laden with Jews being expelled from Spain: as one great center of Jewish life lay in ruins, another was being prepared to replace it. Providentially, the passing of the ships occurred on the Ninth Day of Av, the day of fasting and lamentations over the destruction of the Temple and the day, according to Jewish legend, that the Messiah would come.[28]

There was also a more direct tie between the end of Spanish Jewry and the discovery of America. To escape from the Inquisition, some Jews had joined Columbus' expedition. The physician, the overseer of the crew, and the translator, it was claimed, were of Jewish origin. Moreover, Isabella's financial advisers, who made the expedition possible, were of Jewish lineage. These conclusions were based on the latest research on Columbus by the Budapest Jewish historian, Meyer Kayserling. Commissioned by Oscar Straus in 1891, Kayserling's *Christopher Columbus and the Participation of the Jews in the Spanish and Portuguese Discoveries* appeared in 1894. By 1905, its findings were accepted in Jewish circles as historical truth. When, for example, Rabbi Krauskopf of Philadelphia addressed the New York 92nd Street YMHA on the occasion of the 250th anniversary, *The Times* carried this banner-line: "A Jew First to Land of Columbus's Party."[29] The *Tageblat* presented the same "historical facts" to the Yiddish-reading public: " In the archives of Seville are listed, black on white, the sums of money that the Jew, Luis de Santangel, gave for Columbus' expedition." Probably "half a *minyan* of Jews" were in the discoverer's crew—including the first white man, Luis de Torres, to step on the shores of the New World. "Consequently," the *Tageblat* concluded, "we Jews have a full claim to America and we should not be ashamed to call America our home. . . . We have an [American] ancestry older than all other nationalities, even antedating the English and Dutch."[30] Partaking in the very discovery of America, the Jews were indeed "present at the creation."

The Yiddish press split along class lines in reporting the Carnegie Hall meeting. For the *Tageblat*, "the jubilee celebration was the most magnificent and radiant gathering ever held by Jews in America." All sections and strata of Jewry were present in the packed hall—bankers, merchants, workers, craftsmen, rabbis, statesmen—"and all united in giving thanks for this place of refuge for our homeless and plundered nation." The *Tageblat* in fact printed the texts of the main addresses in the "English Department" of the paper.[31] In contrast, the *Forverts* concluded its account with this observation: "The festivities did not impress one as a people's celebration; besides the wealthy Jewish classes no other class was present. It was a festival for wealthy Jews who gathered to praise God for his benevolence to them." In a long essay, Benjamin Feigenbaum, the socialist firebrand, elaborated on the class theme, turning on end the compliments that Grover Cleveland and others had showered upon the Jews. "The Jewish contributions so praised by the speakers [their enriching the American economy, their individual success, and their respect for the law] had served to strengthen an unjust order that benefitted the millionaires." He continued, "A time will come in America when in speaking of what Jews have accomplished, people will no longer have in mind the great Jewish merchants and bankers but the Jewish masses, the tailors and operators who played a critical role in freeing America from the capitalist yoke." The *Varhayts's* editorial, "Jubilee of the Jewish Bankers," was written in the same vein. It attacked "the people from Wall Street, Madison Avenue, Lexington Avenue, Fifth Avenue, West End Avenue and Riverside Drive" for declaring their celebration "a holiday of the Jewish people" while ignoring the "Jews of Hester Street, Norfolk Street, Ridge Street, Houston Street and East Broadway." More grievous was the festive character of the exercises: "The Jewish masses are not actors. They cannot go out one day with trumpets, cymbals and dance, give thanks to God, and then the next day march in the streets bemoaning the victims of the pogroms." In fact, the *Tageblat* and the Anglo-Jewish press reported not only on the grand celebration, but on smaller events held in immigrant synagogues. For example, *The Times* described an anniversary meeting at the Rumanian congregation Shaarei Shamayim on Eldridge Street, which featured festive speeches and 800 Talmud Torah children carrying American flags marching in a procession led by the band of the Hebrew Sheltering Orphan Asylum.[32]

The Yiddish press played a central role in the third major manifestation of Jewish public culture to be examined here: "der groyser troyer marsh" (the great mourning march) for victims of the Russian pogroms to be held on December 4, 1905. Whereas Shomer's funeral was a street pageant in the tradition of an East European Jewish community honoring a great personage, the 250th anniversary was held in elegant halls and imposing temples, an American creation. The "troyer marsh," a mass demonstration of unity drawing on modern politics and Jewish religious ritual, returned the act of communal bonding to the city's streets. In fact, in early November, the *Forverts* set the tone for what would become repeated calls for popular activism. In a front-page banner headline the paper called, "To Washington! Thousands to Washington! March to the White House! Let the Blood of Our Dead Be Heard." "The greatest catastrophe in Jewish history" had taken place, the *Forverts* editorialized. "If [President] Roosevelt so wished, America could help. How can we make the Jewish voice heard? Demonstrate in Washington." Little came of editor Abe Cahan's call, though later in November several mass marches did take place. In one case, it was the theater unions that organized the demonstration, which concluded with a benefit performance of the play, *Khurbn Kishinev*, (*The Destruction of Kishinev*). In the other instance, the Odessa *landsmanshaft* associations sponsored the march, and in Philadelphia there were organized street demonstrations.[33]

The principal demonstration took place in New York, planned and directed by the newly established Jewish Defense Association. Founded in the beginning of November with the purpose of raising funds to buy arms for clandestine Jewish self-defense groups being formed in Russia, the association succeeded in gaining the participation of broad segments of the downtown Jewish political spectrum. It also had the support of some establishment leaders. From the start of the preparations, the association spoke in the name of Jewish pride, "manhood," and unity. In addition to protest and fund-raising, the association provided the means for fulfilling the mitzvah of remembering and honoring the dead —sisters, brothers, parents—and to shed tears over graves they could not visit.[34]

Critical to the success of the undertaking was the collaboration of the Yiddish press. For six continuous days preceding the march, the Yiddish newspapers published what were in effect "orders of the day," long columns of notices from societies to their members and from the arrangements committee to the societies. All organizations—lodges, labor unions, political parties, *landsmanshaftn* (hometown) associations, and synagogues—intending to participate were instructed to designate an assembly point for their members and to inform the arrangements committee. Musicians and choral groups wishing to offer their services were to contact the committee. Owners of halls and meeting rooms were asked by the arrangements committee to provide them gratis; businesses were ordered to close on the day of the march, and workers were urged to leave their shops and take part. On the morning of the "troyer marsh," the papers published final instructions informing the participating groups where each would gather before joining the march.[35]

The several hundred participating organizations were divided into eight divisions to assure order and efficiency, each headed by a "marshal" who was subordinate to the parade's "grand marshal." The march began at Rutgers Square in the heart of the Lower East Side, snaked through the Jewish quarter and then turned north on Broadway to Union Square. Residents were urged to hang black bunting from windows and fire-escapes along the line of march. The Yiddish press also announced that meetings would be held at eight designated theaters at the conclusion of the march. The published list of speakers, as one would expect, reflected the spectrum of downtown ideologies.[36]

The Times called the march "one of the largest parades this city has ever seen." Thirteen hundred police were required to keep order, although all observers emphasized the decorum of the crowd. According to *The Times*, 125,000 were in the line of march, and a similar number crowded the sidewalks. What stands out in the press descriptions and photographs is the mix of bereavement and protest—of a "phantom funeral" and a military formation—that was symbolized by the flags carried at the head of the parade. The *Forverts* described the red and black banners waving in the wind, the workers' flag and the flag of mourning. (*The Times*' account differed on the last point: "A corps of men carried black banners, American flags and what has become known as the Jewish flag—the banner of Zion—with the blue, six-pointed star of David in the centre." Where the *Forverts* saw red, *The Times* reported blue and white.) Behind the flagbearers came a fifty-person band. Other marching bands were placed at intervals in the line of march. Those who marched in the procession wore black or a crepe around their sleeve or hat, except for the detachments of the Zion Guards from New York and New Haven and the Manhattan Rifles. Banners identified organizations, and large placards in Yiddish—"Mourn Our Dead," or slogans denouncing the czar—were held aloft.[37]

The general press coverage expressed empathy for the demonstration, as the following quote from a *Times's* report indicates:

> The bands between the sections rang out in funeral strains the note of grief [which] were accentuated by similar strains further down the line. Men and women burst into tears, some moved by their losses, others by the dramatic intensity of sound and scene. Occasionally, at a concerted signal, the bands would stop playing. Above the murmur of the moving throng would arise softly at first then swelling to full tone, the voices of the synagogue boy choirs in a hymn for the peace of the dead.[38]

And when the main column approached the synagogues on Norfolk and Rivington Streets, "the procession halted. Bearded rabbis appeared in the little alcoves under the lights and the strangely carved doorways, clasped their hands, prayed for a moment, and then chanted a solemn dirge." When the first division reached Union Square, it filled the park, and it became necessary to proceed with reading the resolutions before all the demonstrators had arrived. One of the resolutions (which carries an uncanny contemporaneity) reads:

> We call upon the Government of the United States and upon all the Governments of enlightened lands to enter their protest against the criminal slaughter of innocent persons, against the brutal massacres which violate all laws of humanity. . . . In the present state of chaos [in Russia] . . . it is the duty of a power like that of the United States to put a halt to the fiendish atrocities.[39]

None of the establishment leaders took part in the "troyer marsh." A letter to the editor of the *American Hebrew*, the weekly they all subscribed to, deplored the absence of uptown Jews in the line of march. Their presence "would have gone far to break down the barriers of caste and class." It was regrettable, the writer stated, that her fellow Jews were unable to overcome their middle class inhibitions that regarded street demonstrations as repugnant and dangerous.[40]

However, the "uptowners" sought other ways of identifying with the protest. Across the land they gathered in their temples on December 4 for memorial services, addresses, and condemnations, urging that even more aid be extended to the afflicted. Furthermore, the Schiffs, Marshalls, and Strauses were working diligently to alleviate the suffering of Russian Jews—lobbying in Washington for diplomatic intervention or sanctions, raising large funds for relief, and coordinating their efforts with world Jewish leaders. Tacitly, the establishment leaders approved of the "troyer marsh" as the justifiable "manly" expression of anger of Russian immigrants for kin fallen victim to marauding hooligans. Moreover, the demonstration was a "success"—massive and orderly—winning the approbation of the general press. In fact, the "troyer marsh" complemented the establishment's political and financial efforts to assist Russian Jews.[41]

One should take note that the "troyer marsh" borrowed much from its American setting. True, the parade had a distinctive Russian Jewish texture. In one respect, it recalled the European funeral procession of a famous personage with eulogies and pauses at synagogues along the route of the procession. In another respect, the flags, slogans, and speeches reminded some spectators of the radical rallies (such as the May Day demonstrations) that, by the late 1890s, were taking place—clandestinely to be sure—in the centers of Jewish socialist activity in the Pale of Settlement. However, the arrangements, structure, and pace of the 1905 "troyer marsh" derived from American practice. The "divisions" and "marshals," the marching bands and flags, the holiday dress of the participants, and the culminating speeches and resolutions in the public square were borrowed from the recently invented May First demonstration, which itself drew upon the German American flair for pageantry. In the first May Day labor demonstration in 1890 (part of the eight-hour day movement), 9,000 Jewish workers participated in the New York parade in what became an annual event. At preliminary meetings in Lower East Side halls, the Jewish cloak-makers, dressed in their finest, listened to speeches and to bands playing revolutionary songs before joining the German and American contin-gents in the march to Union Square. At the square, separate speaker's stands for the German-, English-, and Yiddish-speaking orators were set up in different areas to enable the demonstrators to hear the addresses in their own language. By 1903, the United Hebrew Trades had organized its own supplementary march on the day following the general demonstration with marshals heading divisions and the parade ending at Hamilton Fish Park to hear a battery of Yiddish speeches. Two and a half years later, the experience gained by Jewish socialists in celebrating the international workers' May Day would be added to the experience of the religiously traditional immigrants who mounted the great public funerals in 1902 and 1905 of "Chief Rabbi" Jacob Joseph and the *Tageblat's* Kasriel Sarasohn.[42]

How shall we understand these communal rites that encompassed hundreds of thousands of Jews? In the first place, a handful of notables and communal functionaries and, concurrently, the editors of the Yiddish dailies, orchestrated the commemorative events to meet the needs and sentiments of the Jewish multitudes. At a time when a diffuse and divided American Jewry had almost no organizational core and informal committees of the wealthy and well-connected filled the vacuum in times of crisis, the 1905 celebrations of solidarity advanced the belief in a holistic community. Moreover, they promoted the movement for communal collaboration and the related demand for a publicly recognized leadership.[43] A second, crucial revelation of the 1905 events deserves notice. However dissimilar the public commemorations and demonstrations were—reflecting cultural, ideological, regional, and class differences—they demonstrated a degree of collective self-assurance that was remarkable. The organizers staged their pageants in the public sphere in order to activate, uplift, and educate the Jewish masses; and they paraded Jewish culture, Jewish accomplishments, and Jewish remonstrations before the American people to win its sympathy and respect. This was true even in the most parochial of the three events described above, Shomer's funeral. The immigrant community united in order to display the cultural values it honored. Taking note of this, *The Times* remarked that the immigrant Jews lamented the passing of one of its literary heroes with the same passion and in the same numbers that it had the victims of the pogroms in a protest march only days earlier.[44] Taken together, these pageants of celebration, protest, and sorrow formed overlapping social and cultural orbits. Not all Jews participated in the mass events of November–December 1905. Many were selective in their response. This was to be expected given the varied origins of the Jews who had come to America. But sufficient numbers of Jews did identify with the various celebrations, and thereby helped forge the building blocks of a Jewish public culture.

Public culture is no substitute for the communal web of religious observance, institutional loyalty, ideological commitment, and ethnic fellowship. At best, it supplements a sense of community through participation in the occasional rites of celebration and commemoration. But where the community's institutional life often produced more divisiveness than solidarity, the triad of communal observances that took place in late November and early December 1905 revealed the unifying quality of a public culture in the making. The communal rites and civic pageants considered here, arranged and directed by communal powers, brought American Jewry together, bound it with its past, and provided at least a fleeting measure of collective identity.

The last fifty years have witnessed the rise of an affluent, homogeneous Jewry which is remarkably integrated in American society and culture. The half of American Jewry that, as Salo Baron noted in 1942, did not participate in any form of organized Jewish life has perhaps become the half that marries outside of the Jewish community, causing concern and anxiety for the Jewish communal establishment. For an ethnoreligious public whose sense of self is increasingly marked by ambiguity if not vacuity, the incentive to nurture a Jewish public culture is compelling.

Since 1905, there have been highs and lows in the process of formation of a Jewish public culture that have paralleled the complex interweaving of social and cultural change and the searing events of our times. Israel Independence Day festivities with the parade up New York's Fifth Avenue as its centerpiece, the great 1987 "March on Washington" on behalf of Soviet Jewry, and the opening of the United States Holocaust Memorial Museum in 1993, are some of the well-known benchmarks of this process. Uncovering this history, which requires looking beyond the conventional boundaries of institutional life, can contribute to a deeper understanding of the dynamic history of the communal life of American Jews.

NOTES

1. Salo Baron, "Ghetto and Emancipation: Shall We Revise the Traditional View?," *Menorah Journal* 14:6 (June 1928), 524, 526.

2. Ibid., 526.

3. Salo Wittmayer Baron, *The Jewish Community: Its History and Structure to the American Revolution* (Philadelphia, 1942), I, 25. In a 1952 conference on "Creative Jewish Living," Baron objected to Mordecai M. Kaplan's insistence on the need to establish inclusive "organic" Jewish communities. Baron called the American voluntary community "a revolutionary transformation" from the "secular, national structures of Jewish communities in central and eastern Europe." He noted that in all western countries, outside of Israel, "the Jewish communities are increasingly reshaping themselves along American lines." *The New York Times*, May 18, 1952: 18. See also Robert Liberles, *Salo Wittmayer Baron: Architect of Jewish History* (New York, 1995): 264–265 and Baron's article, "American Jewish Communal Pioneering," first published in 1949 in Idem., *Steeled in Adversity: Essays and Addresses on American Jewish Life* (Philadelphia, 1971), 56–73.

4. Salo W. Baron, *Steeled in Adversity* (Philadelphia, 1971), 457–460, 469–470, from an article first published in *Contemporary Jewish Record*, vol. 5 (1942): 493–507; Idem., "The Modern Age," in *Great Ages and Ideas of the Jewish People*, ed. by Leo W. Schwarz (Philadelphia, 1956), 461–484; Harold Weisberg, "Ideologies of American Jews," in *The American Jew, A Reappraisal* (Philadelphia, 1964), 347–348, Daniel Elazar's *Community and Polity: The Organizational Dynamics of American Jewry* (Philadelphia, 1976) is a comprehensive analysis of the organized Jewish community.

5.   For a discussion of the concept, "public culture," as applied to American history, see Thomas Bender, "Wholes and Parts: The Need for Synthesis in American History," *Journal of American History*, 73:1 (June 1986), 120–136; see the round-table response in *Journal of American History*, 74:1 (June 1987), 112–130. For a suggestive case study of the phenomenon discussed here, see Kathleen Conzen, "Ethnicity as Festive Culture: Nineteenth Century German America on Parade," *The Invention of Ethnicity*, edited by Werner Sollors (New York, 1989), 44–76.

6.   Arthur A. Goren, "Sacred and Secular: The Place of Public Funerals in the Immigrant Life of American Jews," *Jewish History* 8, nos. 1–2 (1994), 269–273.

7.   *Leksikon fun yidishn tiater*, ed. Zalmen Zylbercweig (New York, 1959), vol. 3, 2078–2104; Rose Shomer-Bachelis, *Unzer Foter Shomer* (first part written by Miriam Shomer-Zunzer) (New York, 1950), 122–186; *Tageblat*, 27 Nov. 1905, 1.

8.   *Tageblat*, 26 Nov. 1905,1; *Forverts*, 26 Nov. 1905, 1. For an account of the "elaborate precautions to prevent trouble," see *The New York Times*, 26 Nov. 1905, 12.

9.   See *Forverts* and *Varheyt* for 24, 25, 26 and 27 Nov. 1905; and the *Tageblat* for 24, 26 and 27 Nov. 1905.

10.   *Tageblat*, 27 Nov. 1905, 1,8; *Forverts*, 27 Nov. 1905, 1.

11.   *The New York Times*, 27 Nov. 1905, 9.

12.   *Tageblat*, 27 Nov. 1905, 1,8; Shomer-Bachelis and Shomer-Zunzer, *Unzer Foter Shomer*, 188; *The New York Times*, 27 Nov. 1905, 6.

13.   *Tageblat*, 4 Nov. 1905, 4; Goren, "Sacred and Secular," 272–78.

14.   Ellen Kellman, "Sholom Aleichem's Funeral (New York, 1916): The Making of a National Pageant," *YIVO Annual* 20 (1991), 277–304. On the secularization and politicization of the public funeral, see Goren, "Sacred and Secular," 290–297, where the funerals of the Jewish socialist leaders, Meyer London (1926), Morris Hillquit (1933), and Baruch Vladeck (1938), are discussed.

15.   *The Two Hundred and Fiftieth Anniversary of the Settlement of the Jews in the United States* (published as *Publications of the American Jewish Historical Society* 14 [1906]), v–x.

16.   See Nathan M. Kaganoff, "AJHS at 90: Reflections on the History of the Oldest Ethnic Historical Society in America," *American Jewish History* 91, no. 4 (June 1982), 467–472; Jeffrey S. Gurock, "From *Publications* to *American Jewish History*: The Journal of the American Jewish Historical Society and the Writing of American Jewish History," *American Jewish History* 81, no. 2 (winter 1993–1994), 158–162, 167–171; Naomi Cohen, *Encounter with Emancipation: The German Jews in the United States, 1830.* (Philadelphia, 1984), 249–85.

17. See Michael Kammen, *Mystic Chords of Memory: The Transformation of Tradition in American Culture* (New York, 1991), 93–162, 194–227; John Bodnar, *Remaking America: Public Memory, Commemoration, and Patriotism in the Twentieth Century* (Princeton, 1992), 33–35; David Glassberg, *American Historical Pageantry: The Uses of Tradition in the Early Twentieth Century* (Chapel Hill, 1990), 9–34; John Higham, *History* (Englewood Cliffs, 1965), 6–25.

18. Oscar S. Straus, "Address of the President," *Publications of the American Jewish Historical Society*, no. 1 (Papers Presented at the First Scientific Meeting, Philadelphia, December 15, 1892), 1–4; Idem., *The Origin of Republican Form of Government in the United States of America* (New York, 1885). On Straus' historical writings, see Naomi Cohen, *A Dual Heritage: The Public Career of Oscar S. Straus* (Philadelphia, 1969), 15, 71–73. For interpretations of the origins of the Society that emphasize the American historiographical context, see Ira Robinson, "The Invention of American Jewish History," *American Jewish History*, 81 nos. 3–4 (spring-summer 1994), 309–320; and Robert Liberles, "Postemancipation Historiography and the Jewish Historical Societies of America and England," *Studies in Contemporary Jewry*, vol. 10, *Reshaping the Past: Jewish History and the Historians*, ed. Jonathan Frankel (New York, 1994), 45–65.

19. See Kammen, *Mystic Chords of Memory*, 134–145; Hasia R. Diner, *A Time for Gathering: the Second Migration, 1820–1880* (Baltimore, 1992), 201–202; Barbara Kirshenblatt-Gimblett, "From Cult to Culture: Jews on Display at World's Fairs," in *Tradition and Modernization* (NIF Publications 25 [Turku, 1992]), 80–81; Joseph Guttman, "Jewish Participation in the Visual Arts of Eighteenth and Nineteenth Century America," *American Jewish Archives* 15, no. 1 (April 1963), 44; Richard B. Nicolai, *Centennial Philadelphia* (Bryn Mawr, 1976), 69, 81; Jonathan Sarna, "Columbus and the Jews," *Commentary*, 94 (Nov. 1992), 38.

20. Conzen, "Ethnicity as Festive Culture," 66–69 wherein she cites *The New York Times*, 8 Oct. 1883, p.5 and 9 Oct. 9, 2, for accounts of the parades; Frank Trommler and Joseph McVeigh, editors, *America and the Germans: An Assessment of a Three–Hundred Year History* (Philadelphia, 1985), vol. 1, xi–xiv; H. Arnold Barton, "Swedish-American Historiography," *Immigration History Newsletter* 15 no. 1 (May 1983), 2; Thomas J. Schlereth, "Columbia, Columbus, and Columbianism," *Journal of American History* 79, no.3 (Dec. 1992), 995–960; John Appel, "Immigrant Historical Societies in the United States, 1880–1950" (Ph.D. diss., University of Pennsylvania, 1960), 277–88, 329–34,

21. *The Two Hundred and Fiftieth Anniversary of the Settlement of the Jews in the United States*, v–x, 258–61. Although the first twenty–three Jews arrived in New Amsterdam in September 1654, 1655 was chosen as the anniversary year when the Dutch West India Company overruled Governor

Peter Stuyvesant and granted "a leave of settlement" to the Jews. For an example of the broad support for holding an anniversary celebration see *Jewish Exponent*, 14 April 1905, 7, and 21 April 1905, 4. For criticism that no Russian Jews were appointed to the executive committee, see *Jewish Criterion*, 19 May 1905, 12; *Hebrew Standard*, 5 May 1905, 8, and 12 May, 9; *The American Israelite*, 16 Nov. 1905, 4; *Jewish Exponent*, 24 Nov. 1905, 3, 4.

22. *American Hebrew*, 5 May 1905, 725–731 ; *Boston [Jewish] Advocate*, 19 May 1905, p.1, 2 June, 1 and 7 July, 1.

23. *American Hebrew*, 5 May 1905, 725.

24. *American Hebrew*, 6 Oct.1905, 517; *The Two Hundred and Fiftieth Anniversary of the Settlement of the Jews in the United States*, v–x, 242–258. See Ibid., 199–232 where excerpts from eleven newspapers appear, and the listing in *American Jewish Year Book* 8 (5667–1906/7), 148–166.

25. *American Israelite*, 16 Nov. 1905, 3; 30 Nov. 30, 6; *Reform Advocate*, 2 Dec. 1905, p.2; *Jewish Exponent*, 3 Nov. 1905, 3, 4, 24 Nov. 1905 3,4, 1 Dec., 4,8.

26. *Two Hundred and Fiftieth Anniversary*, ix. For general accounts, see *The New York Times*, 1 Dec. 1905, 1,4, *Jewish Exponent*, 8 Dec. 1905, 9.

27. *Two Hundred and Fiftieth Anniversary*, 34–35, 72–73, 96, 122–123, 127; Emil Hirsh, "Concordance of Judaism and Americanism," *Reform Advocate*, 9 Dec. 1905, 471–474. In his study, *Roger Williams, The Pioneer of Religious Liberty* (New York, 1894), Straus presented the historical case for Williams' support for the readmission of the Jews to England; see 3rd ed. (New York, 1936), 174–178.

28. *The New York Times*, 17 Nov. 1905, 6.

29. *The Two Hundred and Fiftieth Anniversary*, 107–108, 122–127; *The New York Times*, 27 Nov. 1905, 6. On Kayserling, see Sarna, "Columbus and the Jews," 38–41.

30. *Tageblat*, 19 Nov. 1905, 4.

31. *Tageblat*, "English Department," 1 Dec. 1905, 1.

32. *Forverts*, 1 Dec. 1905, 1,4; *Varheyt*, 1 Dec., 1904.1,4; *Tageblat*, 27 Nov. 1905, 1,4; *The New York Times*, 27 Nov. 1905, 6.

33. *Forverts*, 7 Nov. 1905, 1,4, 23 Nov., p.1; *Varheyt*, 23 Nov., 1.

34. See Jonathan Frankel, *Prophecy and Politics: Socialism, Nationalism, and the Russian Jews, 1862–1817* (Cambridge, 1981), 487–92.

35. *Forverts*, 2, 3, 4 Dec. 1905. See also *Tageblat* 29, 30 Nov., 1; *The New York Times*, 29 Nov., 6.

36. *Varheyt*, 4 Dec. 1905, 1; *Forverts*, 4 Dec., 1.

37. *The New York Times*, 5 Dec. 1905, 6; *Forverts*, 5 Dec. 1906, 1.

38. *The New York Times*, 5 Dec. 1905, 6.

39. Ibid.

40. *American Hebrew*, 15 Dec. 1905, 136.

41. See *The New York Times*, 5 Dec. 1905, 7, for an account of the Temple Emanu-El meeting, and Ibid., 6, for a report of the National Committee for Russian Relief's second million–dollar campaign and the report of Jacob Schiff on his diplomatic efforts.

42. Aaron Antonovsky and Elias Tcherikower (eds.), *The Early Jewish Labor Movement in the United States* (New York, 1961), 322–327; N. Goldberg, "Amerikes beytrog zum ershtn mai," *Zukunft* 49 no. 5 (May 1944), 270–271; *Forverts*, 2 May 1903 1; Ezra Mendelsohn, *Class Struggle in the Pale: The Formative Years of the Jewish Workers Movement in Tsarist Russia* (Cambridge, 1970), 137–140.

43. A close examination of the American Jewish public response to the Kishinev pogrom in late April and May of 1903 brings into sharper relief the new phase of collaboration that characterizes the 1905 commemorations. In 1903, the notables of the established community initiated seventy–seven protest meetings in fifty cities across the nation. They were nominally sponsored by "general" committees and featured non-Jewish public figures. (See Cyrus Adler, *The Voice of American on Kishineff* [Philadelphia, 1904], xvii). But the Jewish immigrant public failed to unite in organizing protest meetings, marches, and fund-raising drives. See *Forverts*, 28 April 1903, 1; 30 April, 1; 9 May 9, 4.

44. *The New York Times*, 27 Nov. 1905, 7.

TOWARD A HISTORY OF SCRANTON JEWRY

Michael Brown

In many ways the history of Scranton Jewry conforms to general patterns. Although the colonial (Sephardic) wave of Jewish immigration reached no closer to northeastern Pennsylvania than Easton, the two later waves brought Jews to Scranton as they did to other large and small communities across the United States. Jews came from central Europe in the mid–nineteenth century and from eastern Europe between the 1870s and the closing of the gates of America after World War I. For the most part, Scranton Jews underwent the same processes of adaptation experienced by other American Jews and gentiles. Over time, their ethnic identity became diluted as they moved away from the inner-city areas of first settlement, and their religious observances became at least partially Americanized.

In some respects, however, Scranton's Jews have walked a less traveled path. To a large degree, their fate has mirrored that of the city itself. The community experienced rapid growth and great prosperity in the late nineteenth century and especially during the first three decades of the twentieth. A period of steady decline began with the Great Depression, a decline which has been only somewhat ameliorated by innovative self-help efforts at renewal. Suburbanization arrived in Scranton later than elsewhere; Jews began relocating to the suburbs in significant numbers only in the 1970s. Still in 1996, no major Jewish facility—except for a cemetery—was located outside the city limits; most communal institutions remained within half an hour's walk of the city's downtown business district. Although the community is of modest size (at its height between 5000 and 6500 people), it has maintained a variety of institutions more characteristic of a much larger community: an old-age home, a day school, and a yeshiva (school of Talmudic

135

learning), for example, in addition to the more usual synagogues, community center, clubs, and kosher butchers. And finally, the several factions and denominations which make up Scranton Jewry have managed to live in relative harmony. At the same time, the community has tended to be rather more traditional than many others. At the close of the twentieth century its most vibrant sector was the Orthodox. That group may, indeed, be the only part of the community which can look forward to the future with confidence.

It may be argued that every community is unique and deserves scholarly examination. Local history, moreover, is the stuff of which broad historical patterns are made and against which they must be tested. What Scranton Jewry shares with other communities is, then, certainly worthy of study. But its singular features are of particular interest. An extraordinarily vital, often creative, if small and somewhat off-the-beaten-track, group in an area of the United States with its own peculiar social and economic landscape, Scranton's Jews command special attention. Here it will be possible only to outline some of the contours of communal history and to suggest some areas for future study. The focus is on the religious development of the community, partly because it is the aspect of Jewishness by which most American Jews have identified themselves over the years, but also because the changes undergone by the community over time are well reflected in its religious affairs.

The German Genesis

Jews were living in Scranton before the city was incorporated in 1867. They were among the commercial pioneers of the new city. Kramer's clothing store, established in 1849, was one of the first four stores on Lackawanna Avenue, along the main business street, and it remained a fixture there for some 75 years. In 1851, Jonas Lauer set up shop, followed by other Jews attracted to the growing iron and steel center of northeastern Pennsylvania, including the Samter brothers, who, in 1872, opened their men's clothing store which would remain in family hands for over a century.

Like their brethren elsewhere in the United States then and for many years afterwards, Scranton's Jewish pioneers were not involved in the heavy industries that built the city (iron and steel, coal, railroads, heavy machinery) or in banks or in the city's later major gentile enterprises, such as the International Correspondence Schools and the International

Salt Company. They gravitated to wholesaling and retailing, partly because they had experience with business and little with heavy industry or commercial banking, but also because the gentiles who controlled the banks and big businesses did not welcome Jewish participation in their enterprises.

There were few if any professionals among the early Jews. Arthur Wellington Hart, a transplanted Canadian from a colonial-era, Quebec Jewish family, was an exception. Hart, who fought in the Union army during the Civil War and rose to the rank of colonel, had earlier worked as a newspaper editor in Scranton.[1] Most Scranton Jews of the mid-nineteenth century, however, like those in other American towns and cities, were recent immigrants who came from Orthodox families in central Europe, of humble circumstances, and without much education.

In 1867, just after the Civil War, the thirty or so Jewish families of the city built a synagogue on Linden Street to replace their rented prayer hall which had been located on Lackawanna Avenue upstairs from Green's Liquor Store. (Green was a member of the congregation.) According to the Scranton *Republican*, the new Linden Street Temple of Anshe Chesed Congregation (later Temple Hesed) reflected "a great credit upon the taste and piety of the congregation." Isaac Mayer Wise, the foremost American rabbi of the day and the founder in 1875 of the Hebrew Union College in Cincinnati, was less impressed. In his guest sermon inaugurating the new edifice, Wise described the synagogue as "small and plain when compared with other Jewish houses of worship," a comment which probably did not endear him to the congregation. It is not certain that they took the visitor up on his offer to make the arduous trip to Scranton (then over ten hours by train from New York) for another lecture later that year.

Wise preached in English at the dedication service which was held just before Passover. The rabbi of the congregation, however, Rabbi Weil, who earned the meager salary of $83.33 a month, regularly spoke in German to his immigrant parishioners who were still most at home in that language.[2] Among those parishioners was Simon Rice, the long-time president of the synagogue, whose descendants remained active in the community in the 1990s. Another was Joseph Rosenthal, Scranton's first—and for some years lone—policeman.

Until the 1880s Anshe Chesed was the city's only synagogue. Its members grew increasingly prosperous, and by the latter years of the nineteenth century had assumed the role of local Jewish patricians. By the turn of the century they had put their humble German beginnings and their orthodoxy behind them and were becoming restless in their downtown neighborhood which had by then acquired a large population of immigrant Jews from eastern Europe. Linden Street, the Germans are reported to have grumbled, had become the "*Kugel-Strasse*" (that is, "eastern European Jewish pudding street"). They determined to move "uptown," to the adjacent Hill Section, then populated by well-to-do gentiles: the Woolworths, coal barons like the Jermyns, and others. In 1902 the handsome new Madison Avenue Temple opened its doors in that neighborhood. It would serve the congregation for 71 years.

Until well after World War II, the membership of the Madison Avenue Temple remained small. Eastern European Jews were uncomfortable with the organ, with prayers in English, and with men praying hatless; and the Germans were not particularly eager to have the un-Americanized newcomers in their midst. In the early years of the century, the Temple's rabbi was the New York–born Abraham S. Anspacher, a rather typical representative of the Reform rabbinate of his day. On one occasion Anspacher attempted an outreach program by inviting the members of the Linden Street Synagogue, now sold to Orthodox eastern Europeans, to come to Madison Avenue to light the Hanukah candles together in a public demonstration of Jewish unity. Because the guests insisted, the rabbi and his congregants reluctantly donned hats for the occasion. The experiment was not repeated. The congregation valued its liberation from "old-fashioned" rituals more than it valued unity.[3] In addition to his pulpit activities, Rabbi Anspacher was the founder of Kamp Kewanee in LaPlume, then a country hamlet but now a Scranton exurb. The character of the camp is indicative of the rabbi's Jewish educational agenda. Directed by him and then by his widow and sons, Kewanee mainly attracted wealthy German Jewish children from Philadelphia and elsewhere, including Scranton. (Alfred Rice, Jr., Donny Dembert, Nelson Goodman, and the writer of this essay were campers in the 1940s.) While the campers were Jewish, most of the counselors were small-town, northeastern Pennsylvania gentiles. Sports from wrestling to tennis were the main activities. There was no Jewish programming other than Sabbath services, which consisted mostly of Protestant hymns. After prayers the campers would repair to the dining hall for lunch, which invariably featured baked Virginia ham as the main course.

Despite their eagerness to stand apart from their "benighted" eastern European brethren, Scranton's early German Jews do not seem to have integrated into the gentile community. Blatant antisemitism was not generally a feature of Scranton life in the early years. Still, elite institutions, such as the Scranton Club and the Scranton Country Club were closed to Jews, who were also unwelcome neighbors in the Hill Section and certainly in Green Ridge. In the late twenties, my grandfather purchased a home on Jefferson Avenue not far from the Madison Avenue Temple. When the sale became known, a distraught gentile neighbor offered to buy it from him for several thousand dollars over his purchase price. He sold and used the proceeds to buy a larger house, the former Brooks mansion on Quincy Avenue. Still in the forties, Moosic Lake was a "protected community"—no Jews allowed. And only decades after World War II did the Scranton Club invite Jewish membership. (The original invitees spurned the invitation, recognizing in it an attempt to shore up the sagging finances of the club.) Antisemitism was enough of a brake, then, that until well after World War II, the German Jews mixed mostly with each other. They looked down upon the newcomers; but only rarely were close social relations forged with non-Jews, although some intermarriage did occur.

In 1922, Rabbi Bernard Heller came to the Madison Avenue Temple. Then at the beginning of his career, Heller had already earned a reputation in the Central Conference of American Rabbis, the Reform rabbis' union, as an outspoken traditionalist. He gained mention in *The New York Times*, which was not usual for a Scranton rabbi in the twenties, when he berated his Reform colleagues at a CCAR convention for their lack of authenticity in identifying Judaism with the philosophy of Spinoza and with popular contemporary ideologies.[4] Heller believed Reform rabbis should preach and teach Judaism, not socialism, democracy, or capitalism. In Scranton, he became a well-known public figure writing regularly for the Scranton *Times*.[5] Within the Jewish community he reached out to the Americanizing children of the eastern Europeans. He led Friday evening services in a *tallith* (prayer shawl) with his head covered to make the "downtown Jews" feel at home. So many young people were drawn to the temple that their parents were moved to investigate the new Conservative movement. Heller's congregants were also ambivalent about his success among the eastern Europeans, many of them preferring to keep their synagogue to themselves. The rabbi tried to make his members happy and still be true to himself. Esther Arzt, the wife of the long-time Conservative rabbi in Scranton, Max Arzt, related that one day she met the wife of one of Heller's more influential congregants. "I'm on my way to buy brisket," Mrs. Arzt mentioned casually. "Rabbi Heller is coming to dinner and it's his favorite meat." Her interlocutor's jaw dropped. "But Rabbi Heller is a vegetarian!" she exclaimed.[6] Apparently fearing to offend his "modern" congregants by keeping kosher in public and by not eating in their homes, the young rabbi had let on that he was a vegetarian. Now his cover was blown.

After seven years in Scranton, Heller moved on. Toward the end of his life, he lived in New York near the Conservative Jewish Theological Seminary, where he prayed regularly with his old Scranton friends, the Arzts. Presumably by then he was an out-of-the-closet carnivore. When he died, the childless Heller left the Seminary a large bequest, evidence of his estrangement from the mainstream of the Reform Movement.

The most famous of Scranton's Reform rabbis is the one that got away. In 1915 application for the vacant post of rabbi was made to Anshe Chesed by a graduating student at the Hebrew Union College who had served during his student days in Williamsport, among other places. A son of eastern European immigrants who had grown up in New York's Brownsville section, the applicant was a Hebraist and a Zionist, and one of the finest orators the college had ever produced. The temple, then headed by Frederick L. Wormser, a veteran Scrantonian who served for many years as president of the Scranton School Board and then as the city's director of public safety, turned the applicant down, undoubtedly preferring someone of German origin who was not a Zionist. Eventually the young rabbi secured a position in another coal town: Wheeling, West Virginia.[7] A few years later he moved to Cleveland. There Abba Hillel Silver became perhaps the best-known American rabbi of his day and one of the greatest orators in the United States. As president of the Zionist Organization of America in the forties, he played a key role in the establishment of the state of Israel and was considered as a candidate for its presidency. He survived his rejection by Anshe Chesed, but it is interesting to speculate on what might have been had he gone to Scranton. He would have been a colleague of John Haynes Holmes, minister of the Elm Park Methodist Church, who later became one of America's foremost Protestant clergymen.

If—like many Reform synagogues before the 1950s—the temple tended to be dogmatic in its approach to Judaism and to Zionism, insular, and unwelcoming to Jews of eastern European origin, some of its rabbis and members proved quite responsive to the needs of the larger community over the years. In 1867 synagogue members gave $44.50 to a visiting emissary from Palestine for the relief of Jews there.[8] In 1894 Rabbi Feuerlicht advised A. B. Cohen and others regarding their plan to set up a modern Hebrew school for the children of the Yiddish-speaking newcomers.[9] Forty years afterward, Rabbi Victor Epstein participated in the national welcoming committee for Vladimir Jabotinsky, the firebrand Zionist militant who was the spiritual father of Menahem Begin and Yitzhak Shamir. The YMHA, as the Jewish Community Center was first known, has been the central communal institution since its inception in 1909. By 1920 it had 1100 members; between 1909 and 1945 over 200 groups operated from its premises. Its first building on Wyoming Avenue could not have been built without the aid of Samuel Samter, Charles Ball, and David Landau. And its later building was made possible by the bequest of Myer Davidow, who also gave generously to the Jewish Home of the Friendless during his lifetime. All of these men were Madison Avenue Temple members. Another was I. E. Oppenheim, a native of Aberdeen, Mississippi, and a latecomer to Scranton among the German Jews, arriving only in 1912. Oppenheim, owner of the Scranton Dry Goods, for over fifty years one of the city's two large department stores, played a major role in local Jewish affairs, particularly in fund raising, until his death in 1954.[10]

Finally, here, it may be noted that in the fifties the temple assumed a new character and became much more inclusive. Many of the old families were gone; new members diluted the central European stock. The Reform Movement became more open to tradition; the grandchildren of the eastern Europeans were, in any case, less traditional than their forebears; and Israel became the focus of all Jews' attention.

The Triumph of Conservative Judaism

As noted earlier, immigrant Jews from eastern Europe began arriving in large numbers in Scranton and in the rest of the United States after 1875. Like the established Jews and gentiles, they sought to improve their economic lot and to become Americanized. But while their goals were in some ways similar to those of the German Jews who preceded them, their lifestyle, outlook on life, language, and dress, and religious expectations were different. The Linden Street Temple and its related charitable societies did not meet their needs, and they set about establishing their own institutions.

As time went on, many of these immigrants became Americanized, and their Scranton-born children even more so. (By 1945, 2300 of Scranton's 4900 Jews had been born in the city or surrounding communities, and another 1000 had been born elsewhere in the United

States.)[11] Among the Americanizing element, there was considerable pressure for an expression of Judaism that reflected the American environment, but to which tradition was not a stranger—for a middle ground between immigrant Orthodoxy and German Reform. This they found in the new Conservative Movement.

In September, 1921, Rabbi Alfred H. Kahn of Pittsburgh, was called to Scranton to head the new Conservative Temple Israel. The synagogue had been organized earlier that year by some of the upwardly mobile eastern Europeans, including Louis Hinerfeld, A. B. Cohen, M. L. Goodman, Harry and Samuel Dickstein, and Jacob Levy, men whom *The Argus*, the YMHA newsletter, described as "all fired up with zeal." Their goal, as outlined in the temple's dedication souvenir, was "to establish a modern synagogue which would comply with the thoughts of the American Jew and Jewess, and which would be conducted in accordance with the best traditions of Judaism." Temple Israel's founders hoped to keep their children from joining the Madison Avenue Temple or perhaps abandoning Judaism altogether. But the parents also wanted to break with what they perceived to be the ways of Europe. *The Argus* noted with satisfaction that the new rabbi planned "to organize a Hebrew school of the most modern pedagogic standards," one more appropriate for "a progressive Jewish community" like Scranton, than the "Jewish teaching in the past [which] has been very haphazard." The temple dedication souvenir promised that its "modern Hebrew school" would enable "youth . . . [to] find their way back into the fold of Judaism."[12]

The new temple did not disappoint its well-wishers. The organizers purchased a small church farther up the hill than the Reform temple in what was still considered "a non-Jewish section of the city."[13] They remodeled it several times, and then decided to start over from scratch, erecting a cathedral synagogue with seating in the main sanctuary for over 1000. The building cost $340,000, a very large sum indeed, that reflected the exuberance of the roaring twenties, not the needs of the 183 member families. In 1923 the synagogue engaged a professional cantor, William S. Horn, who would serve for some 60 years; the next year they hired a new go-getting rabbi, Max Arzt, and in 1925 a young, progressive educator named Louis Wolf. It was an impressive professional team.

Although Horn and Wolf would make their careers in Scranton, Arzt, who sometimes described himself as "a miner prophet," would go on to become vice-chancellor of the Jewish Theological Seminary and professor of practical theology there, a well-known scholar of Jewish liturgy, and a member of the Bible translation committee of the Jewish Publication Society. While still in Scranton, he became one of the best known Conservative rabbis in the country. He, too, made *The New York Times*, for comments he delivered at a 1936 Washington convention of the United Synagogue of America, the lay arm of the Conservative Movement. Arzt contrasted "social justice in America with prejudice and persecution abroad." He urged the Conservative laity and all "American Jewry to rally to the support of democracy here."[14] He meant undoubtedly to condemn both communism, which had made inroads among American Jews including those of Scranton, and Nazism. Later, Arzt would be elected president of the Rabbinical Assembly, the Conservative rabbis' union. Locally he served as president of the Council of Social Agencies of Scranton from 1932 to 1934, as a member of the Pennsylvania State Committee on Public Assistance and Relief, a very important body during the depression years, and as a board member of the YMHA, the Jewish Federation, and the Jewish Home for the Friendless (later the Jewish Home [for the Aged] of Northeastern Pennsylvania). The temple professionals were backed by a dynamic group of lay people in the twenties and thirties, including the president of the sisterhood, Pauline Mack, later the national president of Hadassah.

It is said that Arzt made of Temple Israel a "laboratory for synagogue endeavor in many educational areas."[15] As something of an upscale community center, at least at first, it served the needs of a somewhat different slice of the community from those who were attracted to the YMHA. It offered not only a Hebrew school where "the psychology of the American Jewish child" was thoroughly understood,[16] but a junior congregation for youngsters and soon a teenage congregation as well, Scout troops for boys and girls, a sisterhood and men's club, although the latter was never very successful, a choir, and other activities which resembled those of the YMHA.

The temple's most important achievements came in the realm of education. Its Hebrew school and youth programs put Scranton on the American Jewish map, becoming models for synagogues throughout the country. Already by 1923 its Scout troops were regarded as among the city's best. Arzt's successor, Arthur T. Buch, asserted in 1945 that only about 75 of 600 temple adults regularly attended Sabbath morning services. But over 90 percent of temple children, he claimed, came regularly to the Junior Congregation and the Intermediate Youth League.

One should not think that the Messianic era had arrived in the "modern" Temple Israel Hebrew School. Many children continued to rebel against added hours of schooling; and many of the teachers were less than skilled and less than successful. The period just before the present author enrolled in the school was particularly colorful. One of the teachers, Mr. Gitchkill, was renowned for engaging in wild chases, with his pointer in hand, around the room after fleeing pupils. At the end of the week, the harried instructor regularly rewarded his students with Ex-Lax bars. No one is certain whether he knew what they were, but it is more than likely that they represented calculated revenge.

During the period when Louis Wolf was not involved with the school, chaos was more pronounced and less amusing. One teacher, a Holocaust survivor, is remembered for her daily exclamations: "I refuse to teach," exactly the result her pupils wanted. The father of one particularly obstreperous boy appeared regularly to beat up his son at the request of the principal.

Rabbi Buch's successor, Rabbi Simon Shoop, a former army chaplain who would serve the temple for over 40 years, maintained the emphasis on youth. Shortly after he arrived in 1949, the new Hebrew school building was erected, and for the next two decades the temple could boast of very strong youth programs. Scouting rose to new heights under Scoutmaster Bob Roth, who made Troop 65 the highest achieving troop in the city and perhaps the largest, as well. Not only Scouting, but also the junior and teenage congregations, attracted large numbers, including even children from the Reform and Orthodox synagogues. In these years, Temple Israel had a membership of over 700 families, at least half the Jews in Scranton. Rabbi Shoop continued Rabbi Arzt's tradition of community involvement, acting as head of the Israel Bonds Organization and other community groups, and teaching at the University of Scranton and Marywood College; and the temple's lay people rose to leadership positions in almost every organization of the general Jewish community. The temple produced a crop of rabbis: Donald (Nahum) Cohen, Gershon Friedlin, Robert Wolkoff, Jeff Eisenstat, and the present writer, as well as highly committed lay people, some of whom have become pillars of their synagogues in communities across the country.

Dispassionate observers in the mid-fifties believed Conservative Judaism to be synonymous with American Judaism, and not only in Scranton. Hard times for the movement lay ahead, locally because of the economic decline of the city and the departure of many young people, and nationally because of a range of factors that altered the face of the

American Jewish community from the mid-sixties on. But few analysts and almost no participants anticipated those changes in the 1950s.

Orthodoxy Recumbent and Resurgent

While observers and analysts were predicting the lasting triumph of the Conservative Movement in the 1950s, since the nineteenth century they had been predicting the demise of Orthodoxy. Seen by many scholars and lay people alike as the religion of immigrants, of the poor, and of marginal recidivists, Orthodoxy in America was often assumed to be a one-generation phenomenon that would disappear with the last foreign-born Jew.[17] In the early forties in the Flats, the immigrant neighborhood just south of the Central City business district, the vestiges of which were destroyed in the 1955 floods, word among the four- and five-year-olds was that up in the Hill Section, there was a synagogue where the *siddurim* (prayer books) had golden letters.[18] Who could resist the glitter of those letters and who would want to? But these predictions have also proved mistaken, nowhere more so than in Scranton.

As noted earlier, Scranton's first Jews, had been traditional in their behavior in Europe, and even in America to some extent. A. B. Cohen reports that when his group purchased the Linden Street Temple from Anshe Chesed, they found in the building *tallithot* (prayer shawls), *yarmulkes* (skull caps), and *tefillin* (phyllacteries). The Reformers may have felt no need for the traditional appurtenances of prayer in their new temple, but they were not unfamiliar with them. And they could not escape their past easily. As the pioneer Jews were acculturating, the traditionalist cadre in the community was being greatly augmented by newcomers from all over eastern Europe—Litvaks (Lithuanians), Galitzianers (Jews from southern Poland), Hungarians, and Poles.

These newcomers arrived in Scranton during the period of its heady growth. In the years between 1900 and the First World War, Scranton was said to be the fastest growing city in the United States. In 1919 the *National Geographic* claimed that "probably no other city of its class in the world [was] . . . richer than Scranton."[19] During these years the Central City landscape changed radically, with the addition of the Lackawanna Station, the Laurel Line, the Hotel Casey, the Christian Science Church, the YWCA, the Poli Theater (later the Comerford and then the Ritz), and other buildings. Outside the downtown core, the Everhart Museum, Technical High School, and Luna Park were opened.

There seemed to be no end to the prosperity; there was work for all in King Coal's kingdom, including, of course, the Jewish newcomers.

Most of the eastern Europeans were poor and Yiddish-speaking. A few, like H. B. Eisner, were *talmidei hachamim*, scholars in Jewish lore. Others were secularists, Zionists, socialists, anarchists, and communists. They all settled in the Flats and in the downtown area being vacated by the newly prosperous. A few, such as the present writer's grandparents, settled in working-class gentile neighborhoods: the South Side, West Side, and Providence.

A 1904 study of the anthracite coal communities of northeastern Pennsylvania claimed that the Jewish immigrants came as "the poorest of the poor invading our land, but no sooner are they in these [prosperous] communities than they begin to accumulate riches." According to the author, who employed the common stereotypes of the day, Jews were already in 1904 "among the wealthiest in our mining towns," although they were "as filthy as any of the Hungarians . . . and can cringe as low as any [Slav] . . . when soliciting business." More dispassionately, he noted that Jews were engaged as shoemakers, tailors, and plumbers, but mostly as merchants "of some kind or other. The poorest," he remarked, "carry a pack of dry-goods from house to house."[20]

Some of the recently arrived Jews found work in Scranton's burgeoning industries, especially in the garment factories and textile mills, a number of which were owned by Jews then or later. Although they tended to work their way up the economic ladder, as late as 1945, 157 Scranton Jews were employed as factory workers and another two as union officials. And in that year there were still 35 Jewish peddlers and hucksters in town.[21]

However poor they may have been, the eastern Europeans—except for the secularists and socialists—insisted on the amenities of a traditional Jewish life. Peter Roberts remarked, that the Polish and Russian Jews in northeastern Pennsylvania "belong to the orthodox branch of the Jewish faith and carry out with minute exactness the ritual of the orthodox Hebrew. . . . Wherever from ten to fifteen families live," he noted, "there a synagogue is erected, a teacher engaged and the children daily drilled by him in the faith of their fathers."[22] And, indeed, by 1901 there were at least six Orthodox synagogues serving Scranton's newcomers, the members of which differed from each other to a degree in socio-economic status and religiosity, but mostly according to country of origin. In the twenties four more Orthodox synagogues were established: Ohev Zedek (1925) and Machzikei Hadas (1924) in the Hill Section, as well as synagogues in Providence and Dunmore.

For the eastern Europeans, synagogues were not enough. They required kosher butchers and bakers and places to eat, all of which were to be found in Scranton by the turn of the century, as well as Jewish book stores. Now there were orphans to be cared for; and early in the century the Jewish Home for the Friendless was organized. In 1921 the old Weston Estate in Providence was purchased by the community for use as an orphanage and old-age home. Two years later it housed 14 older people and 37 orphans. Later the Jewish Home moved to Harrison Avenue in the Hill Section and then to Clay and Vine; and it came to serve communities other than Scranton.[23]

The most important aspect of Jewish life for the newcomers was schooling for their children. At first education was left to entrepreneurs who set up *hadarim* resembling those of eastern Europe, except that they operated as supplemental schools in the hours after public school. Few of the teachers had training or talent for their occupation. Most were unsuccessful. In 1894, a number of more forward-looking members of the newcomer community, led by the recently arrived A. B. Cohen, determined to reform Scranton's Jewish educational system, or rather lack of it. They succeeded in forming the Montefiore Talmud Torah later known as the Central Talmud Torah and housed at the YMHA. Originally, the school had been named after the English Jewish philanthropist who retired from business at the age of 40 and spent the last 61 years of his life giving away other people's money and his own and doing good works for Jews around the world.

Cohen, who was president of the school until 1925, revolutionized Jewish education in the city by insisting that Hebrew texts be translated into English rather than Yiddish. In his memoirs, he describes how he proved to his colleagues the folly of teaching in Yiddish which the children understood imperfectly at best. One day he went into a *heder* where the children were learning about the tabernacle in the desert. The ark is described in the Torah as ten cubits (*ailen* in Yiddish) wide. Cohen asked the first child what *ailen* were. "Something to hang a picture on," he replied. *Ailen* were unfamiliar; nails, on the other hand, were everyday things. So the ark became "ten nails wide."[24] The story is unquestionably true, but it is doubtful that the children found "cubits" more comprehensible than *ailen*. Whatever its failings, the Montefiore raised the level of general Jewish education in Scranton. And it attempted to reach its charges through such "American" innovations as an annual picnic at Scranton's Luna Park. There the children entered the Temple of Mystery, rode the Merry-Go-Round and the Shoot-the-Chute, and suffered "interesting, patriotic and instructive" programs featuring "prominent speakers [and] rabbis of Scranton and Wilkes-Barre."[25]

Mention should be made here of one of the teachers at the Montefiore, one of the most extraordinary of the eastern European Jews to come to Scranton. Harry Austryn Wolfson was imported by the school in 1905 from New York as a *melamed* (a traditional teacher). An accomplished Hebraist, a poet, and a Talmud scholar, Wolfson boarded with the Levy family and formed a lifelong friendship with David Levy, later a New York psychiatrist married to the daughter of Julius Rosenwald, a member of the family that controlled Sears Roebuck. Wolfson took advantage of the hours when he was not teaching to learn English. In a few months he earned an elementary school diploma at No. 36 School; in the fall of 1905 he entered Central High. Three years later he graduated with what is said by his biographer to be the highest average ever achieved there.

Thanks to the urging of Myer Kabatchnik, an attorney and secretary to the mayor, who was also Scranton's first Jewish Harvard graduate (1906), Wolfson applied to Harvard. There he flourished, first as a student, then as a faculty member, a world-renowned expert on Spinoza and on the Church Fathers. In later years he occupied the first chair of Jewish Studies at Harvard, established for him by the Littauer family of New York. At Harvard, Wolfson, who never married, always welcomed people from Scranton and liked to share with them memories of his time there. One of the high school friends with whom he maintained contact was Clarence Randall, who became president of the Inland Steel Company and a multimillionaire.[26]

Although Wolfson had little opportunity to make an impact in Scranton, other teachers who remained longer, but especially the Orthodox rabbis and leading lay people, did. One of the rabbis was Wolf Gold, who was called to the Linden Street Temple after the German Jews had sold it to the eastern Europeans. Some time after leaving Scranton, Gold became president of the Mizrahi Organization of America, the Orthodox Zionist group. Later he emigrated to what was then Palestine. There he was appointed to the Jewish Agency Executive, and in 1951, three years after Israel gained its independence, he became head of the Jewish Agency Department for Torah Education and Culture. Following his death, Machon Gold, a Jerusalem school for Orthodox women, was named for him.

The most important of Scranton's Orthodox rabbis was Henry Guterman. A very learned Lithuanian Jew who had studied at Slobodka Yeshiva, one of the great nineteenth–century yeshivot, Guterman came to Scranton's Penn Avenue Synagogue in 1909 from Atlanta, where he was succeeded by Rabbi Tuvia Geffen, whose grandson, Rabbi David Geffen, became rabbi of Temple Israel in Scranton some eight decades later. An Orthodox rabbi who was concerned for the welfare of the whole community, Guterman early on earned the respect of Scranton's Jews and was considered the chief rabbi of the city with responsibility for kashrut and for all of the Orthodox synagogues. In his 57 years in Scranton he took a leading role in most important communal activities: the YMHA, the United Jewish Appeal, the Central Talmud Torah, the Jewish Federation, the Hebrew Day School. Impeccably Orthodox and highly regarded by Orthodox colleagues in North America and in Israel, Guterman served as a consultant on *halacha* to the chief rabbinate of Israel, and was written up in *Time Magazine* for having maintained his daily Talmud class throughout his career.

And yet, Rabbi Guterman kept open the lines of communication with all sectors of the community including Conservative and Reform rabbis. His concern for young people straying from the fold led him to experiment briefly during the twenties with late Friday evening services at the YMHA, an innovation which many Orthodox rabbis refused to consider. And although he generally refrained from entering the sanctuary of synagogues which were not Orthodox, he did attend functions in the social hall of Temple Israel, and on at least one occasion, participated in a funeral service in its sanctuary.[27]

Rabbi Guterman's openness and community-mindedness served as guidelines of behavior for the Orthodox community in general. H.B. Eisner, the businessman and Jewish scholar mentioned earlier, discusses in a responsum an intermarriage case in which he was involved in 1900 in Scranton, even before Rabbi Guterman's time. It exemplifies the tolerant approach typical of Scranton Orthodoxy, at least until Rabbi Guterman's death. Although he had some doubts about the issue, Eisner assisted in the conversion of the woman involved to Judaism, recognizing the need to deal compassionately with a painful and distasteful issue.[28] Rabbi Guterman's mature years in Scranton were marked by extraordinary goodwill among all Jewish groups. When he died in 1966, he was mourned by the entire community which recognized that with his passing an era had ended.

During the Guterman years, Scranton Orthodoxy retained

considerable vitality. Although, as noted earlier, scholarly analysts expected the movement to disappear, in Scranton it maintained considerable strength. One reason was that vigorous lay leadership complemented the energetic rabbinic leadership. A number of families, including the Eisners, the Finks, the Harrises, and others, persevered in their commitment to Orthodoxy. That the general community supported traditional institutions reinforced the vibrancy of Scranton Orthodoxy. Undoubtedly, such support was forthcoming, because of the goodwill created by Rabbi Guterman and his laymen. Scranton was one of the few cities in the United States that had a kosher kitchen in a Boy Scout camp. (The only others that can be verified are Brooklyn, Bayonne, and Buffalo.)[29] At two local resorts, Chapman's Lake and Crystal Lake, there were summer synagogues, almost unheard of in so small a community. That Scranton was an exception to the rule of progressive assimilation and diminishing adherence to tradition was illustrated in 1955 when *Life* magazine featured the Fink family as the exemplars of traditional American Judaism.[30]

What is most remarkable about Scranton's Orthodoxy is its postwar resurgence. In 1948, well before many larger communities, local Jews founded the Hebrew Day School. They were in the vanguard of what would prove to be the most significant innovation in American Jewish education. Before World War II, American Jews had been almost universally committed to public schools and supplementary Jewish education. By the 1990s, however, it has been widely recognized that day schools are the optimal setting for offering the kind of intensive Jewish education required for the survival of the community. This was something Scranton's Orthodox community had sensed intuitively long before.

Subsequently the Orthodox group set about establishing other new institutions, most especially the yeshiva. In fact, they were following a pattern well established in Scranton. Since the pre–World War I era, civic leaders had been endeavoring to stave off economic and demographic decline by offering inducements to new businesses and industries to relocate in the "Electric City."[31] Now the Orthodox leaders of the city imitated those successful initiatives and in doing so ensured their survival. While the larger Jewish community, like the city itself, was losing population, the core Orthodox community began to grow. Students came to pursue their education; teachers followed the students; other services were expanded or renewed to serve the educational community. New synagogues were built. And a few new people were attracted to the community because of its Jewish infrastructure and relative peacefulness.

In many locations the Orthodox community followed the path of decline predicted for it. But in Scranton and a few other places in the United States, most of them much larger cities, there has occurred what sociologist Egon Mayer has called a "renaissance of American Orthodoxy." In most of those communities the resurgence of Orthodoxy has been driven by postwar immigrants from Europe who were observant Jews.[32] In Scranton, however, it has been sparked by the activities of far-sighted, native-born Jews. The result has been that by far the youngest and most vibrant sector of the community in the 1990s is the Orthodox group. And it is they who seem to promise the community a future at a time when other Jews are struggling to cope with the inroads of intermarriage and the departure of younger people for more prosperous climes.

For Future Consideration

Little has been said here about the "secular" life of Scranton Jewry. Any understanding of the community requires a serious and full examination of Zionism, the political involvements of Jews, labor and business organizations, and *landsmanshaftn*, as well as fraternities, women's groups, and other social organizations. This is especially the case for the post–World War II period, when religiosity declined and activities relating to Israel became all-consuming. Much more also needs to be said about the religious life of Scranton Jewry, particularly during the later years discussed here mostly with regard to the Orthodox group.

Beyond the tentative explanations already offered, one can identify some other unique features of Scranton which may help to account for its unusually intense Jewish life and interesting Jewish history. They are all points that need exploring and are offered here only in outline:

1. The size of the Scranton Jewish community at its height, between 5,000 and 6,500 Jews, was big enough to permit a variety of Jewish institutions and services, but small enough for cohesiveness. No one could get lost, but the community never had to depend on any one person or small group. Rabbi Buch put it this way half a century ago: Scranton, he said, is "small enough to make each individual count—yet large enough not to make him count too much."[33]

2. The proximity of perhaps another 10,000 Jews in the area

between Hazleton and Carbondale meant that there was a critical mass of people nearby for communal life and potential marriage partners without making the Scranton community unwieldy.

3. The size of the Jewish community relative to the city itself has also been optimal. Jews have exerted enough of a presence not to feel like "the odd man out."

4. That suburbanization occurred late, and even then only partially, has meant that communal cohesiveness was fortified by geographical propinquity, and institutions retained their viability because they were accessible.

5. Although anti-Semitism has not been absent from Scranton life, it has not been a strong driving force. One reason is that Scranton is a relatively new community, one where Jews have been present almost from the beginning of its history. They are usually not considered outsiders as they often have been in communities to which they were latecomers. That has given them a larger stake in their own community.

The foregoing is only an introduction. The full story deserves to be told.

NOTES

N.B. The author wishes to thank a number of people who have been kind enough to furnish him with materials incorporated into the essay or used as background and others who provided the impetus for this study by arranging a talk in Scranton in April, 1995, in which much of this material was first presented. First among these is Rabbi David Geffen of Temple Israel in Scranton. Others include Seymour Brotman, Berenice Brown, Mildred Cantor, David and Aileen Epstein, Dr. Rela Geffen, Norma Harris, Mim Joseph, Sylvia Meil, Abe Plotkin, and Trudy Rice. Thanks are due also to Matthew Brown for suggestions regarding the manuscript.

1.   Frederick L. Hitchcock, *History of Scranton* (New York, 1914), 148. On the Hart family, see Michael Brown, *Jew or Juif? Jews, French Canadians, and Anglo-Canadians, 1759–1914* (Philadelphia, 1987), passim.

2.   Scranton *Republican*, 12 April 1867.

3.   A. B. Cohen, *Memories at Eighty–Five*, 2nd ed. (Scranton: by the author, 1962), 122–24.

4.   *New York Times*, 27 June 1927. See also 25 June 1933.

5. Heller's columns written while he was touring Europe were published in his book, *A Harvest of Weeds or The European Observation of a Peace Advocate* (Wilkes-Barre: Penn Publishing Co., 1924).

6. Esther Arzt, conversation with the author, New York, 1968.

7. Marc Lee Raphael, *Abba Hillel Silver: A Profile in American Judaism* (New York: Holmes and Meier, 1989), 226, n. 1.

8. Ledger of Rev. Loeb Cohen, entry dated Scranton, Pa., July 15, 1867, in the National and University Library, Jerusalem.

9. A. B. Cohen, 55.

10. Ibid., 76–85; *New York Times*, 21 February 1954.

11. Arthur T. Buch, "The Jewish Community of Scranton," DSS dissertation, The New School for Social Research, New York, December, 1945, Tables IV–V, 224–25.

12. "Rabbi Alfred H. Kahn," *The Argus*, September, 1921; *Dedication of Temple Israel, September 11–17, 1927*.

13. *United Synagogue Recorder*, April 1923.

14. *New York Times*, 16 March 1936.

15. *Encyclopedia Judaica*, s.v. Arzt, Max.

16. *Dedication of Temple Israel*.

17. See, for example, Irving Howe, *World of Our Fathers* (New York, 1976), 195–204; Charles S. Liebman, "The Religion of American Jews," in *American Jews, A Reader*, ed. Marshall Sklare (New York, 1983), 259–63; and Howard M. Sachar, *A History of the Jews in America* (New York, 1992), 189–93, 386–90.

18. Related to the author by Dr. Howard Feibus of Potomac, Maryland, 1995.

19. Quoted in John Beck, *Never Before in History: The Story of Scranton* (Northridge, California, 1986), 88.

20. Peter Roberts, *Anthracite Coal Communities* (New York, 1904), 28.

21. Buch, Table VI, 226–28.

22. Ibid., 29.

23. Buch, Appendix C, 192–93.

24. A. B. Cohen, 54–58.

25. "Jewish Day, August 15, At Luna Park," *The Argus*, 1911 (exact date uncertain); Jack Hiddlestone, *Greetings from Scranton: A Picture Postcard Look at Scranton, Pennsylvania, 1900–1930* (Scranton, 1986), 87–89.

26. Leo W. Schwarz, *Wolfson of Harvard* (Philadelphia, 1978), passim.

27. I am indebted to Seth Gross for this information. He told me of Rabbi Guterman's participation at the funeral of his grandmother, Mrs. H.R. Halpern, held in the Temple.

28. Zvi Dov [H.B.] Eisner, *Sefer Hiddushei Ratzda* [Hebrew] (Jerusalem, 5748 [1988]), 89–92.

29. Arnold M. Sleuterberg, "A Critical History of Organized Jewish Involvement in the Boy Scouts of America, 1926–1987," thesis submitted in partial fulfillment of requirements for ordination, Hebrew Union College-Jewish Institute of Religion, 1988, 35–36, 46–47, 88–89, 288–89.

30. "The World's Great Religions: Judaism," *Life*, 13 June 1955.

31. Compare Beck, 114.

32. Egon Mayer, *From Suburb to Shtetl: The Jews of Boro Park* (Philadelphia, 1979), 18, 33–36.

33. Buch, 159.

CONTRIBUTORS

MICHAEL BROWN is Professor of Jewish History and Director of the Centre for Jewish Studies at York University, Canada.

ARTHUR A. GOREN is Russell Knapp Professor of American Jewish History at Columbia University, New York.

MICHAEL L. MORGAN is Professor of Philosophy and Jewish Studies at Indiana University, Bloomington.

DAVID N. MYERS is Associate Professor of Jewish History and Director of the Center for Jewish Studies at the University of California, Los Angeles.

WILLIAM V. ROWE is Professor of Philosophy and Chair of the Philosophy Department at the University of Scranton, Pennsylvania.

DAVID RUDERMAN is Joseph Meyerhoff Professor of Modern Jewish History and Director of the Center for Judaic Studies at the University of Pennsylvania, Philadelphia.

NOMI M. STOLZENBERG is Professor of Law at the University of Southern California Law School, Los Angeles.

INDEX

157